ENQUIRING TEACHERS,
ENQUIRING LEARNERS

A Constructivist Approach for Teaching

ENQUIRING TEACHERS, ENQUIRING LEARNERS

A Constructivist Approach for Teaching

CATHERINE TWOMEY FOSNOT

TEACHERS COLLEGE PRESS Teachers College, Columbia University
New York and London

Published by Teachers College Press, 1234 Amsterdam Avenue
New York, NY 10027

Library of Congress Cataloging-in-Publication Data

Fosnot, Catherine Twomey.
    Enquiring teachers, enquiring learners: a constructivist approach
for teaching/Catherine Twomey Fosnot.
    p.   cm.
    Includes bibliographical references.
    ISBN 0-8077-2980-9. — ISBN 0-8077-2979-5 (pbk.)
    1. Teachers, Training of.   2. Learning, Psychology of.   I. Title.
LB1707.F67   1989   89-12829
370'.71 — dc20   CIP

Manufactured in the United States of America

96   95   94   93   92   91   90   89   8   7   6   5   4   3   2   1

Dedicated to Damien and Joshua
May this book have even a small effect on their education
and the education of their children.

Contents

Foreword

As Fosnot makes clear in this volume, we teach as we have been taught. Most of us were taught from the assumptions that knowledge is to be passed from one person to another, learning ends when an assignment has been completed, simple right answers are the goal, conflict and confusion are to be avoided. Most teaching, therefore, continues to be done from these assumptions, in spite of widespread acknowledgment that our schools are not helping our children understand their intellectual or cultural heritage with any depth, breadth, or sense of value, nor use the imaginative possibilities of their minds.

In contrast, Fosnot proposes and describes teaching that has little to do with the way most of us were taught. She shows adults striving to make their own sense of materials, problems, and issues that are presented to them. It is clear that the adults thrive on this teaching; that adulthood is not at all too late for it. It is clear also that, if the adult is a teacher, having the experience of recognizing the power of her own ideas is likely to have a significant impact on her subsequent teaching. "I feel like a reborn mathematician, and I want my students to feel that way, too," one of her students is quoted as saying.

Fosnot has a marvelous sentence to describe an example from her own early teaching: "I only succeeded in giving him a language for his prejudice." Here was a more dramatic example than most, but it is a characteristic of much of our teaching: it does not change anyone's beliefs. If we fail to give the learners a chance to explore their own ideas and see where they fall short, we are likely to leave their beliefs untouched, and simply give them a language to cover them with. The teaching Fosnot proposes here does not leave beliefs untouched.

Whether we are children or adults, whatever it is that we believe is our only starting point for going on. No matter what our current beliefs, we can always go on to understand better, take our thoughts further, render our ideas more complex and adequate. What a teacher must do is to acknowledge the learners' thoughts and find ways to take them further. This applies whether she agrees with the learner or not, and whether she thinks she has something to learn from this learner or not. Fosnot joins current usage in referring to "misconceptions," but her discussion makes clear that this suggestion of a deficiency model for what could simply be called "the ideas people have at the start" is misleading.

The examples developed here, drawn mainly from math and language, are inventive and full of interest, and they easily engage the reader in taking part in the explorations himself. I would like to have been let in on more of the struggles, though. I miss seeing the productive messiness of teaching and learning.

This book also addresses, admirably, broad issues of the structure of teacher education programs — questioning, for one thing, the current widely proposed idea that one more year of liberal arts courses, taught as they have always been taught, will make better teachers. She proposes a re-structuring both of teacher education and of undergraduate education, and the book can be taken as a welcome call for another Study Commission on Undergraduate Education and the Education of Teachers, similar to the one chaired by Paul Olson, 1970 to 1975, and with a new emphasis. Fosnot suggests that, in general, teachers' undergraduate education, throughout all subject matter courses, should be a preparation for teaching. University teachers should be, in Donald Schon's phrase, "practitioners of reflective intervention . . . [who must] help students reflect-in-action on their learning practice as they might help mature practitioners reflect-in-action on their professional practice" (personal communication, 1980). If this were the approach to all undergraduate education, I can imagine a broad range of undergraduates being captivated by the intellectual excitement of questions concerning what is involved in learning and, by the same token, what is involved in teaching.

What is most welcome about this book is that, while it brings into question several of the central ideas in current educational discourse, it does so through showing us specific steps that have already been taken, on several different levels, in the directions proposed.

Eleanor Duckworth
Professor of Education
Harvard University

Preface

In the last several years, many reports have appeared criticizing teacher-education programs and making various recommendations, from mandating liberal-arts degrees before certification to extending certification programs to five years. The perspective taken in this book is that simply lengthening programs by adding "more of the same" will have little effect. Instead, a thorough overhauling of pedagogical education is suggested, one that empowers teachers to do what must be done in the schools, rather than one that tells teachers what to do.

An empowered learner is defined in this book as one who is an autonomous, inquisitive thinker — one who questions, investigates, and reasons. An empowered teacher is a reflective decision maker who finds joy in learning and in investigating the teaching/learning process — one who views learning as construction and teaching as a facilitating process to enhance and enrich development.

The main question addressed in this book is, What changes in teacher-education programs are needed in order to facilitate such empowerment? I contend that a constructivist approach must be adopted. Chapter 1 provides a rationale for this approach to teacher education, and Chapter 2 delineates the criteria of such a model.

For the last several years, a constructivist approach has been at the core of my work with both inservice and preservice teachers. As a professor at Southern Connecticut State University (SCSU), I am responsible for teaching language arts methods and a course on Piaget's theory and its application to education. Early on, I became disheartened by my students' misconceptions of Piaget's work and by the traditional teaching practice to which I often observed them reverting, in spite of the more innovative practices I knew had been advocated in their methods courses. Consequently, I began to revise both the content and style of my courses. Of primary importance to me in the revision process was the goal of engaging my students in the activity of developmental psychology; I wanted them to learn about this discipline and its application to education by *being* developmental psychologists. Further, I wanted them to reflect on their own learning in the process and to investigate how children come to "know," in order to open new windows from which pedagogy could be constructed and analyzed. As Piaget himself pointed out many times, concepts need to be constructed via action first, before a meaningful label can be attached. Chapter 3 provides a detailed account of sample activities I now use to enable the construction of concepts such as equilibration and self-regulation. Dialogue extracted from various class sessions is also included.

Chapter 4 presents dialogue from writing workshops and spelling investigations. Although I begin working with teachers by involving them as learners in the language arts, eventually, through reflection on their own learning and by investigating children who are learning language, pedagogical principles are constructed.

Chapters 5 and 6 grew out of a project I undertook in 1987, when I took a leave of absence from SCSU to work full time on the Summermath for Teachers program at Mount Holyoke College. Funded by the National Science Foundation, Summermath for Teachers is an intensive two-week summer institute in mathematics pedagogy for elementary and secondary teachers, with staff follow-up provided as teachers begin to implement a constructivist approach to the teaching of mathematics in their classrooms. Directed by Dr. Marty Simon, the program engages teachers in mathematics, as learners, and then uses that experience as the basis for reflection on, and the construction of, a pedagogy appropriate to the development of mathematical reasoning. Chapter 5 includes dialogue taken from videotapes of the 1986 and 1987 institutes for elementary teachers. Chapter 6 presents a case study of one teacher and the mentoring process that followed as she began to implement a constructivist math approach in her second-grade classroom.

Chapter 7 deals with the issue of integration of liberal arts and education. It provides a sample interdisciplinary major and illustrates how education and liberal arts faculty might work together to develop new programs in teacher education. Chapter 8, the last in this book, is an attempt to pull together the various pieces of the constructivist model described in the previous chapters, and to fill in the details of how such a program might really be implemented in its entirety.

Although much of the dialogue presented throughout the book is extracted from various class sessions by use of audio- and videotapes, most names have been changed, and some modifications have been made in order to make certain points and to illustrate a constructivist teacher-education program in action. The major purpose of this book is to depict a program that aims to empower teachers. For that reason, I have chosen dialogue that best represents this process and have edited it to eliminate extraneous material.

If change is to occur in teacher education, the new models advanced must be based on what we know about teaching and learning, and they must aim at producing teachers who are decision makers, researchers, and articulate change agents. My hope is that readers will find the model described herein a viable option for new designs.

Acknowledgments

This book could not have been written without the assistance of many people. The person to whom I perhaps owe the greatest intellectual debt is George Forman of the University of Massachusetts at Amherst, who over the last several years has served as a mentor in helping me to understand Piaget's theory of learning and a constructivist model of teaching.

My students at Southern Connecticut State University (SCSU) and Mt. Holyoke College have been a constant source of inspiration. Their willingness to question and share their thinking openly, their thirst for knowledge, and their excitement over our joint investigations of the learning process formed the basis for this book. One student in particular, Jill Lester, gave graciously of her time, allowing me to document our work together over the course of a year. She then read, discussed, and edited various versions of Chapter 6.

In 1986, Anthony Pinciaro as Vice-president of Academic Affairs at SCSU established a "think tank" composed of faculty members from both education and the arts and sciences, to discuss possible alternatives to a subject-matter major for prospective teachers. The work of this committee formed the content of Chapter 7. My colleagues on this committee (Betsy Foye, Ella Erway, Carolyn Vanacore, Louise Spear, Mike Shea, David Levine, Dave Marczely, Elsa Falls, F. E. Lowe, Bob Gelbach, and Harry Haakonsen) provided insightful perspectives and stimulating ideas regarding teacher education, for which I have much gratitude.

While I was on leave from SCSU, my colleagues at Mt. Holyoke College (Marty Simon, Deborah Schifter, Ellen Davidson, Paula Hooper, Virginia Bastable, Jim Hammerman, and Barry Wadsworth) provided much inspiration. In many ways, my ideas of a constructivist model of teacher education were broadened and solidified by their modeling and insightful discussions. My thanks in particular to Marty Simon, who read portions of the manuscript and offered helpful comments along the way.

Finally, I want to express my gratitude to my family for the support and encouragement offered me during this project. Along the way, my partner and best friend David gave me the courage to persist and assumed more than his share of household chores. My children, Damien and Joshua, were wonderfully understanding of the time demands of the project and the dual pulls of career and motherhood.

Barren Ground

If you want to plan for a year, sow a seed.
If you want to plan for ten years, plant a tree.
If you want to plan for a hundred years, educate people.
　　　　　　　　　　　　　　　— Chinese poet, 500 B.C.

"Tell me what you know about day and night. How do they happen?" Ruth inquired. Jessica, a second grader, was being interviewed by her teacher, Ruth, on the topic of planetary movement. Having just completed a unit on the solar system with the class, Ruth was interested in what Jessica had learned from the variety of activities the class had engaged in, such as making papier-mâché planets and placing them in a simulated orbit, then using a flashlight to show how night and day occur.

"Oh, I know all about it," Jessica responded. "The sun gives us daylight. When we are having daylight, Italy is having night, and then when Italy has daylight, we have night. It happens because the Earth spins on its axis as it travels around the sun."

Complacently assuming she had done a good job teaching the unit, Ruth mused, "Have you ever seen both the sun and the moon in the sky during the daytime?"

Jessica looked puzzled. "Well, yes. I have," she said haltingly. "There must be two moons. Yes, I guess that's right because sometimes the moon is a banana shape and sometimes it is like a ball. Maybe Italy is just having the banana moon when we are having the ball one."

Surprised at Jessica's misconception, Ruth pursued the topic: "But I thought you said that the Earth was spinning on its axis as it moved around the sun?"

"Yes, it is. It's up there moving around the sun," Jessica responded, pointing upward, towards the sun. "That's why we have night and day."

Ruth was incredulous. "But then what is this?" she queried, pointing to the ground below her.

"Silly . . . this is New Haven!" Jessica replied with conviction.

1

Listening to this interview, I was reminded of a similar experience I had my first year of teaching, when 32 smiling third graders depended on me to make their school days meaningful and exciting. I had trained in the 1960s in a program that had as its focus the preparation of teachers with a sensitivity to the needs of inner-city youth; but, because I had married and moved to Upstate New York, my first job was in a very small, rural town composed mainly of farmers and townspeople whose families had lived there for many generations. My pupils were all white and mainly lower to middle class. No matter; I felt it would be as important to eradicate racism there as to teach in the inner city, and my primary desire was to excite children about learning.

The days flew by. I made skill games for children who needed them, abandoned the basals in favor of children's literature, and spent long hours planning ways to make the days rewarding to the children.

One day a black child from a neighboring town visited a friend in another classroom. I overheard some derogatory racist comments made on the playground by my children and determined that something need- ed to be done. The next unit I meant to cover in my social studies curriculum was Brazil. I decided to abandon it and do instead a unit on black history.

For the next month, the children studied the history of blacks in the United States, through the trials of slavery, rebellion, and the Civil War, as well as the lives and contributions of some famous black Americans. I was proud of my unit. I felt it was much more relevant to my students than a unit on Brazil would have been, and I hoped by developing a pride and respect for black Americans I would be eradicating the preju- dicial views some of my third graders held.

Several months later, the Harlem Ballet Company toured the state and gave a guest presentation at the elementary school where I was teaching. During lunch, several of the dancers joined the children in the cafeteria. Bobby, one of my more immature third graders, came run- ning up to me, shouting, "Teacher, teacher, there's a slave in the cafete- ria!" I was mortified!! How could Bobby have so misunderstood the unit? I had tried to undo prejudicial thinking, and instead it seemed I had actually worsened the situation. Rather than changing his thinking, I apparently had succeeded only in giving him a language for his preju- dice.

After several years of classroom teaching, I realized something that now seems obvious. Learners, in an attempt to make sense of new information and experiences, transform and organize in relation to their own meaning bases. Of utmost importance to good teaching is the ability to probe the understanding of the learner; to be aware of developmental issues; in a sense, to be skilled in the art of "getting inside the student's head." In order to have a better understanding of the way in which children think, I eventually returned to graduate school as a doctoral student in early childhood education, studying specifically Piaget's work and its application to the classroom.

Five years later, armed with all my new learning and an Ed.D., I took a position on the faculty of an institution engaged mainly in teacher preparation. One of the courses that I was assigned to teach was called "Piaget for Teachers." I was most excited about this course, since the content was my field of expertise and I believed vehemently that teachers needed to understand development and its effect on children's thinking.

I spent approximately half the semester lecturing about Piaget's theory, believing that students couldn't begin to apply it in classrooms until they understood it. I placed special emphasis on Piaget's notion of equilibration, explaining assimilation as an active process of making meaning out of experience, and accommodation as the changing of one's own thinking in order to strive toward equilibrium. Next I moved on to explain developmental differences in the way children assimilate by describing the typical Piagetian tasks and the way in which logical reasoning changes from preoperational thinking to eventual formal operational structures. Finally, I defined constructivist teaching as a model that emphasizes that learners need to be actively involved, to reflect on their learning and make inferences, and to experience cognitive conflict. During the second half of the course, I explained several ways Piaget's theory applies to education by describing some sample lessons. I even described some examples similar to the earlier related scenarios with Jessica and Bobby and explained assimilation in light of the examples, following with pedagogical solutions.

On the surface, my course seemed to be just the missing link for beginning teachers like Ruth, but today I know a deeper look is needed. This realization hit me full force one day when I overheard one of my students proudly telling a friend how she was applying Piaget's work in her teaching practice. She had made a puzzle that was self-correcting, since the pieces would only fit under the category in which they belonged, and she was using it with her preschooler in order to teach classification. Rather than reflecting on Piaget's tasks and protocols as examples of how children think, and seeing the beauty of how children's logic is inventive and changes with development, she was simply using reinforcement theory to produce classification behavior. In fact, she seemed to have missed totally my emphasis on construction and the importance of letting children invent. To put it in Eleanor Duckworth's

(1987a) words, she had forgotten the importance of facilitating "the having of wonderful ideas."

I began to listen carefully and probe for understanding with my graduate students, just as I had learned to do with young children many years earlier. Several misconceptions soon became apparent. First, like the student previously described, some assumed they needed to teach conservation and classification. Second, some construed cognitive conflict as negative reinforcement and began to try to provide an external contradiction rather than facilitating an internal one, respecting self-regulation. Third, some missed the difference between experience and constructive experience and assumed that if learners were manipulating concrete materials they must be learning. In a few cases, the misconceptions were so strong that I even began to wonder with trepidation if some students were leaving the course with a more damaging view of how to teach than when they entered. In my worst moments I questioned whether I might be one of those incompetent teacher educators who had been criticized by several recent reports (Carnegie Forum, 1986; Holmes Group, 1986; A Nation at Risk, 1983).

I've come to believe, instead, that there is a deeper, more fundamental connection between teacher-education programs and children like Jessica and Bobby. This link is the implicit assumption that permeates the thinking of educational institutions as well as mainstream society, namely, that knowledge is a case of having more facts and information, that more knowledge changes behavior, and that people need facts and information first in order to think. I had originally believed I could change racist thinking by giving my students more information about black history. Although I had come to recognize the naïveté of that position, I had only repeated the mistake with college students by assuming that if I taught Piaget's theory to preservice and inservice teachers, they would apply it in their classroom teaching.

A second, even worse misconception exists, that teaching is telling, and that the art is in communicating well. Teaching is never telling, because learners transform what is told to them as they make associations to what they at present know. Their present logical structures also organize the information told to them into meaning units, in order to make sense out of it. Jessica was unable to understand planetary movement from a heliotropic view, since she still held a geocentric view of the universe and further had not yet constructed the class-inclusion relationship of New Haven as part of Earth.

These problems are endemic to all institutions of education, regardless of level. Children sit for 12 years in classrooms where the implicit goal is to listen to the teacher and memorize the information in order to regurgitate it on a test. Little or no attention is paid to the learning process, even though much research exists documenting that real understanding is a case of active restructuring on the part of the learner (Piaget, 1976, 1977, 1980). Restructuring occurs through engaging in problem posing as well as problem solving (Karmiloff-Smith & Inhelder, 1974), inference making and investigation (Fosnot, 1984), resolving of contradictions (Inhelder, Sinclair, & Bovet, 1974), and reflecting (Fosnot, Forman, Edwards, & Goldhaber, 1988; Steffe & Cobb, 1988). These processes all mandate far more active learners, as well as a different model of education than the one subscribed to at present by most institutions. Rather than being powerless and dependent on the institution, learners need to be *empowered* to think and to learn for themselves. Thus, learning needs to be conceived of as something a learner does, not something that is done *to* a learner.

Teachers may be producers of passive learners, but they are products of the system as well. Not only did they sit for 12 years in elementary and secondary classrooms learning how to regurgitate what teachers wanted, but they refined these skills in college with approximately 3 more years of liberal arts education.

According to Hay (1984), a factory model of education exists today as a residue of the Industrial Revolution. The educated learner is conceived of as a product. Students are assessed originally for lacks or needs, then drilled until skilled. The content of what should be learned to be an educated person is assumed to be universal, therefore all learners receive the same curriculum and educators attempt to achieve equality in outcome of product. An empowered learner in this model is both unwanted and dangerous.

Society today, however, is in major transition. As we move out of the Industrial Age into a new era dependent on technology and service, the idea of creative, analytical, empowered learners is far more attractive. Industry points out that the tasks of computing and writing a decent sentence with correct spelling can easily be performed by technology. More important is the ability to think critically and creatively, brainstorm, work cooperatively with others, synthesize, organize, and think abstractly. Hay (1984) pointed out that if you hold an industrial age definition of intelligence based on the belief that the percentage of knowledge of information in your field that you hold stored in your head equals an intelligence quotient, then with the quantity of new information being discovered today, you're getting dumber by the minute!

Most information today can be accessed easily with computer technology. Knowing where to go for it, how to organize it and synthesize it, and how to manipulate it constructively become of prime importance. Deep understanding of concepts is needed for such thinking. Success alone is not sufficient; in fact, Cleveland (1986) argues that real-world problems of today cannot be solved by single disciplines of knowledge alone. Breadth of knowledge, integration of disciplines with a deep understanding of the structure of thinking within them, and insight into the connections and dialectics among subjects are viewed by Cleveland as the hallmarks of the "educated."

With these changing demands of society being placed on the schools, it is not surprising that teachers, schools, and teacher-training institutions have come under widespread criticism, each in turn for failing at its mission. In an attempt to defend itself, each has adopted measures of accountability, ranging from achievement tests in the elementary schools to competency-based teacher education on the university level.

This move toward accountability has worsened the situation rather than helped it. Since assessing true understanding of concepts is far more difficult than assessing simple computation or factual knowledge, simpler knowledge such as facts and application tend to be assessed more abundantly. Goodlad (1983), in *A Place Called School*, states that 75 percent of testing done is for recall of information. Teachers, under pressure from administrators, teach toward the goal of high test scores. Rather than deeper understanding, only superficial knowledge is achieved as teachers attempt to "cover" the curriculum. On the university level, supervisors may spend up to half of their supervisory time documenting visits and filling out competency checklists on students, rather than using that time for the "real" business of teacher education.

Is the point of this discussion to excuse these failings of schools of education? Not at all. The vicious cycle must be broken somewhere, and it may as well start with schools of education. But change will not be simple. As Murray (1986) states,

> Reformers have . . . recommended that attention be given to such ideas as increased subject-matter competence, more standardized testing, the addition of a fifth year to teacher preparation programs, differentiated career opportunities, increased clinical experience, higher salaries for teachers, and the like. But few of the reformers have seen that these issues are interrelated and more complex than each by itself would suggest, because each by itself could become a superficial and symbolic reform that could actually worsen the problems it was meant to solve. The current reform proposals will fail, as they have in the past, because they attempt to reform education simply by telling teachers (and everyone else) what to do, rather than by empowering them to do what must be done. [p. 29]

Murray's (1986) main point, that teachers need to be empowered as thinkers, is an important one. Today's system of education does not facilitate such development. Instead, teachers are viewed as passive recipients of knowledge to be imparted. Like sponges, they are expected to soak up a wealth of information from the liberal arts. Since they are responsible for all subjects, elementary teachers in particular are expected to have up-to-date information in science and social studies, as well as an understanding of the deeper structures of mathematics, and be skilled in the finer aspects of the language arts. Yet, because they do not major in any of these fields and thus miss out on the higher-level seminar courses, they rarely do any intensive thinking in these areas and much of the information they are required to learn is often outdated before they teach it. Teachers are left feeling both overwhelmed with the amount of information in each field and incompetent to teach these disciplines.

In education courses, preservice teachers are again bombarded with information, this time from the field of education. Diagnostic tools, learning deficiencies, learning styles, methods of motivation and reinforcement, developmental processes, methods of evaluation, curriculum design, models of instruction, and materials and tools for teaching are all explained. With this "wealth" of information, preservice teachers are then placed with a "master" teacher for at most a semester, more frequently eight weeks, with the expectation that by the end of the designated period, the role of the "master" teacher will be assumed by the novice. Little or no time is spent as a teacher/researcher or problem solver in the designing of curriculum to meet learners' needs. Instead, emphasis is placed on the emulation of the master teacher's style and the smooth implementation by the novice of the master teacher's program.

Eventually preservice teachers graduate and apply for their first positions in the public school domain, where they are immediately faced with the pressure of accountability. Little or no support for veering from the curriculum or established modes of instruction is given. Such veering, even when it fails, might allow teachers to gain, firsthand, an understanding of developmental processes in relation to a sequence of concepts to be taught and possible methods for integrating them. Instead, teachers are reinforced for efficient "covering" of the curriculum, smoothly managed classrooms, and skilled imitation of clichéd ways of teaching. Teachers' energies are spent on imitating rather than on thinking.

Concerned with improving the schools, some reformers even support a refinement of this model. Research on effective teaching (Berliner, 1986; Brandt, 1986) asks school districts to designate their most competent, skilled teachers and then studies them to find out what they do. The characteristics and behaviors thus isolated are held up as the ones to be inculcated in teacher-education programs. (Imagine, if you will, a program for training scientists that was based on studies of past scientists' behaviors and encouraged novice scientists to copy these behaviors. Would science ever advance?) Doesn't it make more sense to spend time determining what creative teaching could be and then figure out how to get there?

A similar criticism is also made by Romanish (1987). He points out that while school-effectiveness researchers appear to have documented the need for a strong leader, that need appears only because of the way in which researchers have framed their questions. He suggests that "if authority rested with a team of researchers, students, parents and administrators, the research perhaps would show that an effective school has an effective leadership team" (p. 10); and he proposes we look at Waldorf schools, which have no building principal at all.

The mentor model, newly suggested by the State of Connecticut, is another example of a teacher-education program that offers little in the way of empowering teachers. Under new state legislation, prospective teachers are no longer certified by institutions of higher education. Instead, after completing only 30 credits (including student teaching) in education on the undergraduate level (since an undergraduate liberal arts degree is mandated) or, even worse, only a 60-day "wonder" program in the summer after the completion of a baccalaureate degree in the liberal arts, preservice teachers are hired by the public schools. A mentor (another classroom teacher in the school) is assigned to oversee and guide the novice through the first year of teaching. A state team then evaluates and recommends this new teacher for certification (or determines not to recommend, as the case may be). Not only does this system lengthen the course work where teaching is construed as "telling," but it provides little or no time for fieldwork where trial and error can occur under the guidance of university personnel. In addition, with stakes as high as certification, little innovation or exploration in teaching behavior will occur. Instead, novices will be expected to imitate skillfully the present mode of instruction prevalent in the school. A situation of perpetuation of common practice will exist, rather than critical and creative thinking.

In essence, autonomous thinking in present-day teacher-education programs is squelched, and then teachers are criticized for not being able to think. Proposed solutions are to "teach teachers how to think" by offering course work in thinking per se, or by mandating a liberal-arts degree and the passing of a basic competency test in the skills of writing and math (Carnegie Forum, 1986; Holmes Report, 1986).

These proposals are based on an erroneous assumption that more effective education is going on elsewhere in the university, and they only nibble at the more fundamental problem. Citing the work of Jones (1975), Simon (1985) reminds us that research has shown that, in spite of the efforts of teacher-education programs, teachers are much more likely to teach as they have been taught throughout their schooling than as they have been taught to teach in teacher-education programs. Teachers, themselves, are products of an outdated educational system. In the words of Smith (1980),

> Make no mistake about it, adding a course here and a course there, reshuffling academic requirements, screening candidates for admission, integrating methods courses and student teaching, or adding an internship will have little effect upon the ability of teachers to cope with demands upon them now made by the growth of knowledge, new social conditions, and a consumer-oriented public that knows what it wants only in general and abstract terms. Nothing short of thorough overhauling of pedagogical education will do. [p. 87]

With a case made for major pedagogical change and with teacher-education programs cited as the place to begin, the important question becomes, What changes in teacher-education programs are needed in order to have far-reaching repercussions on the education of our children?

2

Seeds

At first, there were colorless, green ideas.
— Gardner, *The Mind's New Science*

I'm reminded of a conversation, told to me by a friend, that occurred at the dinner table with his parents many years ago. He was telling his father, who held a Ph.D. in political science, of his desire to go to medical school. His mother, just tickled to hear that her son wanted to be a doctor, said, "Oh, that's wonderful! We'll finally have a doctor in the family." Her husband looked at her in amazement. "Well, a *real* doctor, I mean," she said, apologetically. "You mean," he retorted, "you're going to send your son to a trade school?!"

TEACHING: VOCATION OR PROFESSION?

The Classic Battle

This dialogue is representative of the classic battle that has been waged for years between the "liberal-arts elitists" and the "vocational technicists." Nowhere has this battle been waged more fiercely than in the field of teacher education. Although some educators have attempted to compare their field to a new science, analogous to psychology, many liberal-arts communities have attacked it as less rigorous and more vocational in its aims. Others, even within the ranks of education, have viewed the main mission of teacher education to be job procurement. Such confusion has often placed departments of education in precarious situations. According to Beyer (1986), conflict over the aims of education has oftentimes resulted in teacher education being segregated from other disciplines and valued only in its ability to secure employment for its candidates.

A historical perspective sheds some light on the evolution of this battle. According to Haskins (1923), the early concept of the university was as "a home for scholars." Disciplines were united (hence *uni*versity) as scholars took on the role of learning and transmitting classical knowledge. The "ivory tower" was indeed one, as it remained lofty and separate, almost a haven, from the everyday problems of society.

In the nineteenth century, research in chemistry, biology, and medicine began to have an impact on the definition and role of the university (Beyer, 1986; DeVane, 1957). This expanded role into research reached a climax by the turn of the century, when universities attempted to answer the research needs of government, industry, and the general public. By the twentieth century, universities consisted of separate disciplines, each involved in separate pursuits and activities (Barzun, 1968; Beyer, 1986).

The development of land-grant universities brought about the final change. Through the Morrill Act of 1862, the needs of the common citizen were taken into account and "many universities became committed to such innovative ideas as education for the working class, practical education in the pursuits and professions of practical life, experimentation and research, the college reaching into the community through institutes and lyceums, and opportunities to study in almost any subject" (Beyer, 1986, p. 38). It was within this climate that departments of education were added. Reciprocally, many normal schools of education expanded to become universities.

Education, a field that has aspects of all the various historical movements, became a battleground. While the foundations of education encompass the traditions of history, philosophy, and sociology and as such are reminiscent of the early university focus, the research paradigm comes from the sciences, that is, psychology, biology, and the physical sciences. Yet, the field is grounded by practical application. With this diversity within the field, it is not surprising that it meets with a crossfire of political and social aspirations.

The Corporate Influence

In the 1980s, the vocational perspective has gained a firm foothold with the rise of a powerful force: the corporate influence. This factor has already had major effects on the practice, aims, methods, and evaluation tools used. Romanish (1987) points out that it is

> not merely following business interests [that] causes the schools to be conservative in character, but more important is the schools' penchant for following a business ideology in the conduct of their affairs. School personnel speak in terms of their "product," "delivery systems,"

"school plant," "needs assessment," "time on task," and "management by objectives." Teachers are "classroom managers" and there is an all consuming preoccupation by the system with "quality control." [p. 11]

The involvement of business in the current reform process is further evidence of its influence. There have been more business representatives than classroom teachers on blue ribbon commissions; in fact, classroom teachers are conspicuously absent. The National Commission on Excellence in Education (NCEE), in preparing its analysis, *A Nation at Risk* (1983) gave only one slot out of 33 to a classroom teacher. The Holmes (1986) and Carnegie (1986) commissions have pressed for an increased voice and status for teachers, yet Carnegie has not a single classroom teacher on its task force, and Holmes is dominated by deans and others (Romanish, 1987).

Even the message of much of the reform is economic in basis. As Goldberg and Harvey (1983) point out in their analysis of the NCEE report, it states that the "nation is at risk because competitors throughout the world are overtaking our once unchallenged lead in commerce, industry, science, and technological innovation" (p. 15). The Carnegie (1986) report contained a similar rationale. Romanish (1987), in a critique of the corporate influence, concludes that *A Nation at Risk* was "a manifesto for vocational education. It marked a fundamental shift from an industrial to a technological focus, but its purpose was to retool public education in order to meet the corporate demands of emerging economic conditions" (p. 11). He further admonishes that the "personal needs of students and the democratic needs of our society . . . are at risk if education does not tend to them" (p. 11). While there has been little criticism against using schools to serve Wall Street, Romanish poignantly makes us aware that "if the AFL-CIO, national farmers' organizations, or the Pentagon were to do so, their efforts would be seen for what they were and condemned" (p. 11).

The Resolution: Encouraging Empowerment, Creativity, and Professionalism

True reform in teacher education will not succeed until the battles over its aims and goals are resolved. Taking a vocational, corporate perspective narrows the scope of our vision and produces institutions that value product over process; trained and skilled technicians over empowered, creative thinkers; schedules and time on task over flexibility and inquiry; and competition over cooperation. Under a corporate umbrella, accountability becomes supremely important, producing teachers who blindly follow "teacher-proof" materials and preset curricula. Teachers, having had little experience in higher-level thinking themselves, are at a loss as to how to develop this ability in their students.

Successful reform, instead, mandates going beyond the vocational, corporate view to a case of developing empowered intellectuals who can respond flexibly, critically, and creatively to the needs of the learner in relation to the needs of society. For reform to last, teachers will need to be able to act as articulate, potent change agents in an arena ripe for change but entrenched in traditional and outdated modes of existence. To meet the demands of this role, teachers need to be educated as professionals, rather than as technicians; as critical and creative decision makers, rather than as skilled imitators.

ALTERNATIVES TO THE TRADITIONAL LIBERAL-ARTS APPROACH

A model of teacher education that shows promise in developing empowered professionals is that of the "teacher as researcher," advanced by Duckworth (1987a). By research, Duckworth is not referring necessarily to empirical, experimental research, but to field research with children along the lines of anthropological research. She proposes that preservice and inservice teachers need to question and research children's understanding of concepts, then reflect on the logic used in reaching such understanding. She further suggests that preservice teachers need to have "their own world opened" (Duckworth, 1987b) by being encouraged to pursue their own investigations in content areas such as science, mathematics, and the language arts. As their own intellectual focus becomes one based on inquiry, teachers develop an understanding of how to encourage inquiry in children.

When prospective teachers are continuously engaged in inquiry about children's understanding and about pedagogy, they develop the ability to probe astutely children's thinking and to understand and appreciate developmental differences, and they become keenly aware of the need for active investigation by learners themselves. Prospective teachers who have been taught to question and construct creative, possible solutions will be empowered as professionals and will be able to facilitate such empowerment of children.

This model is a far cry from the "skilled-practitioner" model prevalent in most teacher-education programs today. Romanish (1987) argues that "the educational system itself is paralyzed by structural features that prevent policy makers from envisioning such fundamental reforms. The policy makers' reality consists of schools as they are currently organized, and the visions embody a narrow gaze of teaching itself" (p. 9). To develop a critical vision, he suggests, in line with Goodlad (1983), that teacher-education programs need to separate teachers from what they have come to perceive teaching to be.

Although most reformers have recognized the need for teachers to be involved in higher-level thinking, a liberal-arts degree has usually been advanced as the solution. Both the Carnegie (1986) and Holmes (1986) reports recommend that teacher education become a five-year program with a bachelor's degree in arts or sciences achieved along the way. In fact, some states (i.e., Connecticut and California) now *require* a liberal-arts major for certification. The problem with this solution, as Newport (1983) points out, is that extending the training period for teachers with just "more of the same" might actually increase the adverse effects of many of the current problems of teacher education.

In 1987 the State of Connecticut mandated a basic competency test in mathematics and language arts for all students entering education programs. The minimum amount of prior liberal-arts education before the test was taken was 14 years (including elementary and secondary school and 2 years of general liberal arts on the college level). Many of the students in fact already had completed 4 years of liberal-arts undergraduate work previous to applying to education departments. In the spring of 1987, almost half of the students who took the exam across the state did not pass it! These data suggest that more liberal arts, taught in the same way, should not be viewed with optimism as a solution to the problems in teacher education. If 14 years of traditional schooling have not developed basic competencies in math computation and writing skills, should we expect a few more semesters of the same to make a real difference?

Instead, these data, coupled with the fact that teachers teach as they were taught rather than as they were taught to teach (Goodlad, 1987; Jones, 1975), suggest that a new, drastically different model of teacher education is needed in order to develop "teachers as researchers," teachers as empowered professionals. Two requirements, in particular, immediately become obvious: (1) the need for a fruitful integration of teacher education with liberal arts, whereby courses are team taught and prospective teachers are given the opportunity to be learners in classrooms where content, learning, and pedagogy are interrelated; and (2) the need for a heavy concentration by prospective teachers on field research into children's understanding. These two topics will be the focus of the remainder of this chapter.

TEACHERS AS LEARNERS: RATIONALE FOR
AN INTEGRATED APPROACH

Perhaps the most potent way to provide experiences where preservice teachers are engaged first in inquiry about content areas and then in reflection on pedagogy is the combining of some of the liberal-arts content courses with methods courses in each area, team taught by liberal-arts and education faculty. Just adding reflection on pedagogy is insufficient, however. These courses need to be designed from an experiential base with emphasis placed on concrete, active exploration and investigation in the content area. For example, mathematics and science courses need to be problem based and inquiry oriented. Writing courses need to be workshop based.

Several reasons can be given for recommending such integration. First, as previously mentioned, research by Jones (1975) points out that teachers tend to model their own practice on the methods used to teach them when they were youngsters. For example, if teachers were taught science through a textbook, lecture, and demonstration approach for most of their years of schooling, although they may have been taught about the need to teach it through a discovery, hands-on, process approach in their methods courses, most will revert back to what their earlier teachers did. This finding should not be surprising, given that a large body of research exists (e.g., Bandura & Walters, 1963) conclusively demonstrating that learners imitate the social behavior of role models held in high esteem.

Second, liberal-arts faculty have much to gain from working with education faculty. While they have usually spent years studying their disciplines, most have spent little time studying the learning/teaching process. Thus, most liberal-arts courses tend to be taught in a lecture/discussion style, with good teaching equated with clear communication, rather than with the promotion and facilitation of learner-centered inquiry and investigation.

Reciprocally, education faculty, while they have known for years how to teach for empowerment, have rarely employed these techniques in their classes. According to Howey (1983),

> One could logically expect that teachers of teachers would employ a wide variety of teaching technologies or methodologies. However, in general, instructional diversity is limited. The Preservice Study reports that the lecture/discussion format is still far and away the dominant teaching modality employed. There appears, in fact, to be a diminishment in the use of other instructional approaches which have been widely applauded. [p. 13]

Jones (1975) makes a similar point:

> A student [prospective teacher] needs as role models not only teachers
> of children whom he can observe and work with, but also his own
> teachers. . . . In most colleges this is a rare experience. We are far
> more likely, as college teachers, to lecture and give examinations (the
> role we were socialized into by our own college experience) about
> . . . theory and methods than to take the risks ourselves of providing
> a laboratory experience. [p. 34]

The writings of Jones (1975) and Howey (1983) point out that what
has existed in most teacher-education programs to date has been a case
of "Do as I say, not as I do." Instructional methods such as individualiza-
tion, responding to different learning styles, moving from the concrete
to the abstract, and using various questioning techniques are all discussed in education courses, but how many of these techniques are
actually used by the instructor in the teaching of the information?

Team-taught, integrated content and methods courses provide
teacher educators with the opportunity to use, themselves, the techniques they espouse. Instead of lecturing to prospective teachers about
what they should do in order to engage children in high-level thinking,
educators have the opportunity to engage preservice teachers in the very
same process, using tasks, problems, and discussions on their level, related to the content they are learning.

Modeling, from this perspective, is not to be construed as a passive
learning tool, the sole desired result being imitation by the learners.
Instead, modeling is used to engage the preservice teachers in experiences that are meaningful and confront their traditional schemes of
teaching with new techniques and methods. Thus, the main purpose of
the modeling is for critique, analysis, and debate of pedagogy. In this
way, prospective teachers are engaged as learners, *along with* education
and liberal-arts faculty, in a "community of discourse" (Beyer, 1986)
aimed at developing a pedagogy of action. This type of experience serves
as a constructive experience for the teacher candidates and involves
them in critical, creative thinking about pedagogy. Since they are actively questioning and investigating techniques of instruction, they become empowered, "thinking" teachers, rather than teachers who rigidly
follow a cookbook approach to instruction.

Philosophical Foundations for Integration

Integration of liberal arts and education has been advocated before, and to say that it is difficult to achieve (given the classic debate

between the liberal-arts elitists and the vocational technicists) would be an understatement. The "teacher-as-researcher" model, however, resolves this debate and provides a new focus.

Phronesis.   An interesting proposition that supports such integration and provides a philosophical basis for this model has been advanced by Beyer (1986), who asserts that education needs to be reconstrued as "practical philosophy," along the lines of the Aristotelian notion of phronesis. The basic idea undergirding phronesis is that truth and certainty are value-laden and illusory and thus cannot serve as a basis for any field. Claiming that the nature of knowledge, certainty, and objectivity have come under widespread debate in the liberal arts, Beyer (1986) cites four principles from Kuhn's classic, *The Structure of Scientific Revolutions* (1970), as proof. The first is that scientific work only takes place within the operation of some paradigm that has its own distinctive set of assumptions, beliefs, techniques, and facts. Second, since such paradigms are necessary, no paradigm can be seen as objective, nor can it be judged. The third principle is that disciplines are interwoven and inseparable since they are united by paradigms of study. This provides the basis for the fourth: Because a paradigm necessarily involves theories, facts, and values in matrices that cannot be separated, there are no such things as theory-free, objective facts or data.

Epistemologists such as Rorty (1979) and Comfort (1984) have contemporaneously supported Kuhn's (1970) position. Comfort (1984) writes: "The hard-hat model of an objective reality has had to yield to a growing perception that the objective is, in form at least, a construct: what we appear to see is a function of the manner of seeing (hardly a new idea to Greek philosophy), but with the awkward complication that the cogitating I arises from the structures which it sees and orders" (back cover).

Beyer (1986) suggests that, since knowledge as certain, objective fact is a questionable premise, an argument over the credibility of education as a science and as a viable intellectual endeavor is a fruitless one. Instead, he asserts, the fields of liberal arts and education ought to join together to form "communities of discourse, committed equally to reflection, conversation, and action" (p. 41).

Empiricism.   Similar criticism in relation to the objectivity of knowledge is being leveled at empiricists in the field of education. Empiricism is defined by *Webster's* as "the theory that all knowledge originates in experience." Generally, empiricists hold that knowledge is a copy of a world exterior to the self; stimuli affect the learner and are processed. Each experience or observation adds to prior ones, and knowledge is thus the total of observations the learner has had. No a priori thought on the part of the learner is assumed. Empiricism is frequently equated to logical positivism, which holds that all meaningful statements are either analytic or conclusively verifiable, or at least confirmable by observation and experiment.

Empiricism in education takes the form of reductionism, or preplanning a curriculum by breaking a content area or skill into assumed component parts or subskills and then sequencing these parts into a hierarchy ranging from simple to more complex. It is assumed that observation or experience at each of these sublevels will quantify to produce the whole, or more general, encompassing concept. Further, learners are viewed as passive, in need of motivation, and affected by reinforcement. Thus, before they even meet their students, teachers spend their time developing a sequenced, well-structured curriculum and determining how they will assess, motivate, reinforce, and evaluate their learners. Children are simply tested to see where they fall on the curriculum continuum and are then expected to progress in a continuous, quantitative fashion. Child development may be considered, but only in terms of the sequence of the preplanned bits or subskills.

Bloom's (1976) mastery learning model is a case in point. It is based on the assumption that wholes can be broken into parts, that skills can be broken into subskills. Learners are diagnosed as to the level or subskill needed, then taught until mastery is achieved at each level. Further, it is assumed that if mastery is achieved at each level then the more general skill encompassing the parts has also been taught.

Most elementary and secondary schools today take an empiricist/reductionist approach in their curriculum planning. Fields are isolated and categorized as if they were really separate entities (e.g., science, math, reading), and then they compete with each other for time in the overall curriculum. Subskills are identified and sequenced into preplanned curricula. Learners are diagnosed, motivated, reinforced, and posttested. Again, we see the role of the teacher as a technician who assesses the needs of the learner and then presents the "correct" prescribed sequence of objectives in the "correct" instructional mode. Even the teacher gets evaluated. Not only are the students' test scores used to validate what they have learned, but in some circles they are even considered an appropriate measure of the teacher's performance! The implicit assumptions are obvious: Parts add up to wholes, and variables can be controlled and isolated, given enough information and appropriate measuring tools.

A recent study in the Chicago public school system (*New Haven*

Register, 1985) found an empiricist/reductionist educational technology to have some problems. The Chicago schools adopted a mastery learning approach in their K–6 reading instruction programs. Subskills such as beginning consonant sounds, vowel sounds, ending consonant sounds, consonant blends, vowel digraphs, and comprehension were taught in a structured, sequential manner until mastery was achieved at each level. Teachers found that in the first few years of the program reading achievement scores increased. By sixth grade, however, an interesting fact was observed. Although reading scores were high on achievement tests, upon entering junior high, reading levels decreased. In fact, learners actually were found not to be reading! A research group brought in to study the problem found that the tests were only measuring what had actually been taught, that is, the subskill or component part covered. Learners, in fact, were spending most of the allotted language arts time completing dittoes or workbook pages related to these subskills, but they were spending only a few minutes a day actually reading. Although they had mastered each component skill in isolation, they were still not reading for meaning, enjoyment, or information.

Constructivism. When the empiricist educational technology has been attacked on practical and theoretical grounds (e.g., Fosnot, 1984, 1986; Koetting, 1984; Nichols, 1987) a constructivist approach frequently has been offered as an alternative (see Fosnot, 1984, 1986). Constructivism can be defined by the following four principles.

1. *Knowledge consists of past constructions.* Philosophically, constructivists assert that we can never know the world in a "true," objective sense, separate from ourselves and our experiences. We can only know it through our logical framework, which transforms, organizes, and interprets our perceptions. Furthermore, this logic itself is constructed and evolves through development as we interact with our environment and try to make sense of our experiences. In essence, cognitive development comes about through the same processes as biological development — through self-regulation or adaptation.

2. *Constructions come about through assimilation and accommodation.* Piaget (1977), one of the most renowned constructivists, breaks self-regulation into two polar (though intimately connected) processes: assimilation and accommodation. Assimilation simply refers to the logical framework or scheme we use to interpret or organize information. When this assimilatory scheme is contradicted or found to be insufficient, we accommodate; that is, we develop a higher-level theory or logic to encompass the information. We adapt and alter our old concepts.

In the case of Jessica (in Chapter 1), we saw that she assimilated quite well the activities from the unit on planetary movement. She transformed, organized, and interpreted them within the context of her own logical framework. Since she had not yet moved away from a child's egocentric perspective, she could not imagine herself turning in space, and she knew the ground did not move underneath her! Hence, she saw the Earth as being above her, moving around the sun — a logical conclusion. Until this egocentric, assimilatory scheme is contradicted, she will continue to use it to organize and transform experiences and information.

3. *Learning is an organic process of invention, rather than a mechanical process of accumulation.* In contrast to empiricist/reductionist approaches, learning in the constructivist model is not seen as an accumulation of facts and associations. Rather, it is believed that structural leaps in cognition are made throughout development, producing qualitatively different frameworks of understanding. Although the maturationist view also subscribes to such stages, it assumes that they just unfold automatically. A constructivist takes the position that the learner must have experiences with hypothesizing and predicting, manipulating objects, posing questions, researching answers, imagining, investigating, and inventing, in order for new constructions to be developed. From this perspective, the teacher cannot insure that learners acquire knowledge just by having the teacher dispense it; a learner-centered, active instructional model is mandated. The learner must construct the knowledge; the teacher serves as a creative mediator in the process.

4. *Meaningful learning occurs through reflection and resolution of cognitive conflict and thus serves to negate earlier, incomplete levels of understanding.* Neither contradiction nor cognitive conflict should be equated with negative reinforcement. They do not stem directly from feedback but instead also are a construction of the learner. Let us return again to Jessica. When she negates her egocentric perspective, her understanding of planetary movement will be qualitatively different than the one she holds at present. At a point where two contradictory schemes become apparent to her, cognitive conflict will arise. Perhaps she will develop the construct of class inclusion and realize that New Haven is part of the Earth. Whatever scheme she constructs, it must be a contradiction to her earlier one, in order to bring about disequilibrium. Again, the teacher can only mediate this process.

Summary: Creating a Community of Discourse

The fact that both education and the liberal arts are engaged in a discussion on the objectivity of knowledge suggests that members of both groups might be able to join together, as proposed earlier, in a "community of discourse" (Beyer, 1986) within a common paradigm.

Constructivism and phronesis have much in common. Both share the belief that knowledge is constructed in the process of reflection, inquiry, and action, by learners themselves, and thus must be seen as temporary, developmental, and nonobjective. Both insist that ideas, principles, and theories are not immutable and purport instead that energies be spent in discourse, action, and reflection. These perspectives suggest that, rather than dispensing a list of prescribed methods of instruction to preservice teachers for their use, these teacher candidates themselves need to be immersed in an environment where they are engaged in questioning, hypothesizing, investigating, imagining, and debating. They need to be part of a community that actively works with them as *learners* and then allows the experience to be dissected, evaluated, and reflected upon in order for principles of pedagogy and action to be constructed.

TEACHERS AS FIELD RESEARCHERS

While reflecting on the learning experience and questioning and investigating pedagogy with faculty are important, they are not sufficient to produce competent teachers. Of primary importance is field research with children. Clark and Lampert (1986), in an analysis of studies on teachers' processes, describe a need for thinking and behavior that are contextual, interactive, and speculative. By *contextual*, these authors mean that teachers must be able to think on the spot, in relation to the context of the problem and the social climate of the classroom. They provide the following explication:

> The decisions teachers make are situation-specific, and they must take into account the aspects of the immediate situation that make it different from any other case. The circumstances that might suggest a particular route toward a goal can be wholly different from one moment to the next. At the same time, teachers need to know about the whole, both temporally and spatially (Doyle, 1977). What one decides to do today has a great deal to do with what happened yesterday and what effects such a decision will have tomorrow, next week, and next month. [p. 29]

The *interactive* aspect of teaching, according to Clark and Lampert (1986), relates to the way in which teachers "work at establishing a culture in which there is a shared understanding of what is happening and where it is leading. . . . They negotiate with students to ensure their membership in that culture" (p. 29). When teachers ask questions of students, listen to responses, and probe for understanding, they are engaged in an interactive "dance" of facilitation and negotiation of learning (see Fosnot, 1988).

Finally, the methods used and decisions made are not preplanned, rigid, and fixed, but instead are *speculative* and hypothetical in nature:

> What we have learned about teaching requires us to define teacher knowledge as speculative. There is a great deal of uncertainty in the teacher's work; a teacher chooses or rejects an exercise in the textbook, a particular seating plan, or a way of speaking to a child in the hope that it will produce the desired outcome. . . . Their thinking is, of necessity, hypothetical and probabilistic. The knowledge they use is tentative, subject to change, and transient rather than fixed, objective, and unchanging. [Clark & Lampert, 1986, p. 29]

Thinking characterized as contextual, interactive, and speculative in nature can only be developed by extensive fieldwork in classroom settings as well as with individual children on a tutorial basis. All through the education program, regular opportunities need to be created where teacher candidates can research children's understanding and then design and try various instructional approaches, while critiquing and evaluating their successes. At least four types of field research experience are envisioned: investigative, cooperative, reflective, and integrative.

Investigative Field Research

An investigative field experience is problem based and involves inquiry, exploration, problem posing, and problem solving. For example, on a one-to-one basis, a teacher candidate may meet with a child and try to discover, in relation to a given concept, what a child knows about it. Through probing and the use of "clinical interviewing" (see Labinowicz, 1985, for a good description of Piaget's clinical method), the schemes and misconceptions may be uncovered. During the process of investigation into the child's understanding, the teacher candidate continuously hypothesizes about where the misconceptions may lie and explores the child's reasoning, using various tasks and counterexamples. The research problem is "solved" when the candidate feels confident of a diagnosis. Although some testing may be used, the point here is neither to ascertain traditional grade-level scores nor to assess competencies and skills. Instead, it is a chance for teachers to learn how to explore, listen, and investigate children's reasoning and understanding. Piaget (1978) has clearly demonstrated that success on school tasks is not analogous to real understanding, yet, because teachers are usually trained to assess only competency on tasks, understanding is frequently sacrificed. This type of field experience is important in that it gives teachers first-hand experience in exploring *how* children think and may in fact raise many important questions about the validity of standardized testing and the need for alternative types of evaluation.

A second type of field investigation entails working with a small group of children, or again on a one-to-one basis, to test out various strategies and methods for teaching certain concepts. In this way the teacher candidate critically explores children's needs and plans creative solutions to teaching problems. The strategies implemented are discussed with faculty, videotaped, and critiqued in seminar. The focus here is not on evaluating the teacher's performance, but on providing the opportunity for exploration, problem solving, creativity, and real pedagogical decision making.

Investigative fieldwork needs to take place early in the program. As Friedman, Brinlee, and Hayes (1980) point out,

> Because of the separation between coursework and fieldwork, teacher educators have often left it up to students to figure out how to apply the concepts covered in a course. . . . The distance, both in time and place, from the students' actual "need to know," made relevant applications difficult. . . .
>
> Without provisions for integrating the academic and the field components of teacher preparation, what could have been useful learning experiences remain simply experiences. Sitting in a ninth grade classroom for X number of hours will no more prepare one to be a teacher than sitting in an operating room will qualify one to be a surgeon. While this exposure may help the prospective doctor and teacher develop more realistic expectations of their future roles, we should not thereby assume proficiency in the removal of either an appendix or ignorance. [p. 10]

On the other hand, if education courses consist of seminars based on investigative fieldwork, prospective teachers have the opportunity to develop, with the support of faculty, the type of thinking so aptly described by Clark and Lampert (1986). Teacher candidates are more likely to be explorative and inventive when the environment is less stressful, such as teaching in microcosm in the teacher-education classroom or with small tutorial groups of children. Also, the pedagogical solutions and strategies tried are in relation to specific children's needs, rather than to the successful implementation of a set curriculum. This focus

allows prospective teachers the opportunity to gain an in-depth understanding of the curriculum needs of the child and thus may serve to
develop their ability to evaluate prepackaged curriculum materials critically.

Cooperative Field Research

Cooperative fieldwork relates to a full-time team-teaching situation in a model school environment. This situation maximizes the opportunity for teacher candidates to apply the methods, skills, and
knowledge that they acquired in their teacher-education seminars and
to extend them to a full classroom.

Although this type of fieldwork may appear similar on the surface
to the traditional student-teaching experience, it is distinctly different in
that it is cooperative in nature, rather than imitative. In the traditional
student-teaching experience, students usually begin with small-group
work, are responsible for designated lessons, and then eventually take on
the role of the master teacher with responsibilities for the whole class.
The expectation exists that the student will be able to carry on the work
of the master teacher smoothly and in a similar fashion; hence the
situation is imitative.

The perspective advocated here is instead a cooperative venture,
where students brainstorm, plan, and implement together *with* master
teachers. Again, the focus is on creative and critical thinking in relation
to pedagogical decision making. Cooperative field research gives teacher candidates the opportunity to gain, in a supportive environment,
knowledge in relation to management issues, scheduling, planning, and
curriculum development, as well as further abilities in contextual, interactive, and speculative thinking (Clark & Lampert, 1986). It also extends the period where creative trial and error can occur and thus
deepens the candidate's understanding of the teaching/learning process.

Of utmost importance, in order for the goals of cooperative field
research to be realized, is the choice of sites used. According to Risley
(1986), the presidential commission that was formed to respond to *A
Nation at Risk* (1983) has suggested that certain public schools be identified to work with universities as model sites. This fits in well with the
expressed purpose of cooperative field research. If certain schools were
identified and were willing to try innovative methods, then "portal
systems" could be developed and utilized. "Portal systems" refers to
university extension sites where a group of teacher candidates could be
placed together for field research, so as to provide a support system for
each other. Seminars could be held on site by university faculty, in

conjunction with the staff of the school, addressing the needs of the school as well as the needs of the teacher candidates team teaching there. University faculty might also do demonstration lessons while on site. In this way, the university would give to the community its expertise, as the public school would, in turn, give to the university.

An important contribution to the aims of cooperative field research would be the use of teacher-education faculty to teach in these "portal" public school classes (Simon, 1985). Such an opportunity allows teacher educators to demonstrate their methods with children and makes additional, appropriate classroom environments available for fieldwork experiences; but, most important, it provides an important sabbatical experience for education faculty. It is too easy for university faculty to lose touch with the real world of the classroom. If, every few years or so, university faculty were encouraged to spend a semester teaching in a "portal" school, their knowledge base of classroom experience would be updated and refreshed. Such an experience also provides an opportunity to the school for new methods to be tried on site.

Reflective Field Research

The third type of field research is reflective in nature. The idea for it stems from the work of Armstrong (1980) and Rowland (1984), two British teachers. Both had been teaching elementary youngsters for several years when they decided to combine the roles of teacher and researcher in order to investigate the quality of children's intellectual understanding and its growth. Rowland continued teaching, and Armstrong joined him in his class for a year, observing closely the learning of the children and reporting his observations in a book, *Closely Observed Children: The Diary of a Primary Classroom* (1980). The book documented and analyzed the painting, writing, and explorations of a number of the children in the class. Rowland (1984) became very involved in and excited about Armstrong's research, writing,

> From my experience of working on my own in a classroom, I had begun to realize that whenever I looked really closely at what the children were doing, the choices they were making and the forms of expression they were using, then a picture began to build up of a child who was, in some sense, more "rational" than I had previously realized. It seemed that, the closer I looked, not only the more I saw, but the more intelligent was what I saw. . . . It was those occasions when I was able to reflect sufficiently to provide some understanding of why the children worked in the way they did, that motivated me as a

teacher. A few such insights into their learning were worth more than
a battery of objective measures of their performance. [pp. 4–5]

A few years after Armstrong did research in Rowland's classroom,
the latter decided to conduct fieldwork himself, alongside another
teacher in another school. He was interested in the issue of learners'
autonomy, the possibility or desirability of children exercising some control over their activity. Specifically, he wanted a clearer understanding
of what this autonomy amounted to, how children could make use of it,
and how it might serve to develop his own approach to teaching. After a
year of study of children learning in the classroom of a teacher in
Leicestershire, Rowland wrote a book called *The Enquiring Classroom*
(1984), which documented his observations.

What is striking about the work of both Armstrong and Rowland is
the insightful and potent conclusions they draw from their observations.
Their books both offer astute, important illustrations for teachers, as
well as providing a new model for the evaluation of teaching. Rowland
(1984) writes,

> This concern to understand the children is not merely an attempt to
> evaluate whether or not a teaching objective has been successful (as in
> the "examination"), but is a fundamental aspect of the interaction
> that takes place between teacher and learner as they learn together.
> The meaning of the knowledge, skills and experience involved in any
> teaching/learning act is not defined by the teacher alone, but is open
> to a process of reinterpretation as the children attempt to relate the
> experience afforded them to their existing knowledge. It is through
> such processes of reinterpretation, as teachers and learners strive to
> understand each other, that we gain some access and insight into the
> children's understanding. It is in this way also that we can evaluate
> the effects of our teaching. [p. 4]

The focus of reflective field research, as envisioned here, is similar
to the type of research conducted by Armstrong (1980) and Rowland
(1984), although briefer. Students who have completed their cooperative research experience would stay in the portal system for a semester,
to partake in reflective research. This would entail in-depth focused
reflection on a pedagogical issue of interest to the teacher candidate,
culminating in a synthesis paper. For example, students might choose to
do a critical analysis of K–6 children's writing, or to study the development of the concept of fractions, functions, or number.

Observational work is not new to traditional education programs;
however, it usually occurs in the beginning of the program. Teacher
candidates, at that point in their careers, have little notion of what to

look for and thus often gain little from their observation. This is why reflective field research needs to occur after the initial teaching experience, when prospective teachers have deeper, more insightful questions that they need to pursue and can use as a focus for their study.

Reflective field research not only gives candidates the opportunity to study in-depth questions related to knowledge or learning, but also may develop the ability to evaluate the teaching/learning situation. Faculty supervisors have traditionally done all the evaluating. Student teachers have been asked to design and implement lessons and have been assessed as they performed. Reflective field research engages them in the evaluation process instead by having them observe other teachers involved with children in a learning situation. When prospective teachers have their own classrooms, they will be engaged in frequent evaluation and monitoring of the learning process. In fact, as previously discussed, teaching entails constant modifying and regulating, as learners and teachers interact. According to Neely (1986), reflection on one's own thinking (cognitive monitoring) in relation to the learning process is a potent determinant of planning and implementing better lessons. What better way to gain an ability to assess learning than to spend time doing a focused analysis during reflective fieldwork?

Integration

Integrative fieldwork is the culminating activity of the preservice education program. It is conceived of as a year of teaching one's own class (a paid position), but as a clinical fellow rather than a fully certified teacher. This proposal exists in practice in other clinical fields already: Doctors do residencies; speech pathologists and audiologists do clinical fellowship years (CFYs). The main difference between clinical fellows and certified teachers is that fellows still receive support from the university.

The rationale for a CFY comes from the work of Joyce and Showers (1982). These researchers found that when only theory was presented to teachers in workshops on instructional innovations, 10 to 20 percent of the participants acquired an understanding of the innovation, but only 5 to 10 percent applied it. When theory presentation plus modeling were used, 35 percent acquired an understanding and 5 to 10 percent applied it. When practice of the innovation was added, 70 percent acquired an understanding of the innovation, but still only 5 to 10 percent applied it. Even when feedback was added to the practice sessions, although 80 percent of the participants seemed to have a thorough understanding of the innovation, only 5 to 10 percent applied it in their classrooms. The only condition that made a distinct, significant difference in application was coaching through the following year. With coaching, 80 to 90 percent of participants applied the innovation. These data suggest that, for real change to occur in practice in public school classrooms, supportive coaching must be given during the stage of beginning implementation. Otherwise, innovations may be tried but will usually fall by the wayside as teachers revert back to old, more comfortable schemes of teaching.

During the clinical fellowship year, a university faculty member visits the teacher's classroom once a week as a resource, a coach, and at times, if the teacher desires, a demonstrator of innovative practice. In this way, the new teacher is provided with a transitional experience and is given time to gain confidence and knowledge before being evaluated for certification, which is granted after the completion of a successful CFY. Although this plan assumes that public schools will be allowed (and be willing) to hire clinical fellows, this proposal seems justified in that the possible inexperience of the fellow should be compensated for by the faculty member acting as coach/resource.

SUMMARY

With this discussion of field research, Chapter 2 comes to a close. Two criteria have been identified as necessary in a preservice education program that aims toward the development of teachers as empowered researchers. First, it is important for the aims and goals of education to be clear and unified. Combining the philosophy of phronesis and the tenets of constructivism may yield a fruitful relationship between liberal arts and education faculty. Bringing these faculty together in "communities of discourse" engaged in "reflection, conversation, and action" (Beyer, 1986, p. 41) once more unites the *university* in a common goal — education of its nation's people. The establishment of a community of discourse provides prospective teachers with experience *as learners*, which can then serve as a focus for reflection, debate, and evaluation of the pedagogical principles and decision making involved. In this way the emphasis is placed on developing questioning, thinking teachers, empowered because they will be constructing their own beliefs about pedagogy by reflecting on their own learning process, rather than passively imitating a model.

Second, field research has been discussed as the necessary core of a program and four types of field research have been proposed: investigative, cooperative, reflective, and integrative.

In this chapter only the "seeds" of a program have been presented. While they may at present be only "colorless, green ideas," the next several chapters fill in the details by presenting specific examples of possible courses and programming and, where appropriate, excerpts from protocols of preservice or inservice teachers involved at present in such programs.

3

Green Ideas Grow:
Investigations in Psychology

*Educational experience that sensitizes participants to the
existence of personal construct systems and creates an
atmosphere of inquiry will lead to an awareness of self as
functioning as an everyday scientist — thus potentially
enhancing one's own freedom of action and understanding.*
— Sigel, "Constructivism and Teacher Education"

In revising my course, Piaget for Teachers, I hoped to establish a community of discourse through the processes of activity, reflection, and conversation. I had come to realize that, for students really to understand Piaget's concepts of equilibration and self-regulation, they had to experience them firsthand. Toward that aim I currently begin my course by engaging my students in an experience that I expect will engender some disequilibrium.

TEACHERS AS LEARNERS:
CONSTRUCTING PIAGETIAN CONCEPTS

Equilibration

John, a seventh-grade teacher in a private school who was enrolled in the certification program at SCSU, was explaining his approach to the following problem: If you bicycled up a hill at 20 mph, then turned around and bicycled down at 60 mph, what was the average speed traveled from start to finish? His reply was, "Well, if you want to find the average speed traveled, you just add the speeds traveled together and divide by the number of trips."

It was the first night of class, and the 30 inservice and preservice teachers enrolled had been presented the problem and asked to work in groups of three to solve it. They had been told that the groups were responsible for making sure that each member could explain the solution and prove the answer. While the students were working, I moved around the room listening to the reasoning going on in the groups. Several groups were quickly adding 60 and 20, then dividing by 2, ending with an answer of 40 mph.

I joined John's group and asked the members to explain to me their solution. Joanne explained that the rule for averaging was to add the parts together, then divide by the number of parts. They had done that and gotten 40 mph as an answer. I asked where their divisor, 2, had come from, and Steven, the third member of the group, replied, "That's the number of parts . . . *two* trips."

"Are the trips equal in duration?" I queried. The group then seemed puzzled and unsure of an answer. I left them as they began discussing whether the duration of the trip made a difference or not, and moved to another group.

This second group had decided that adding the two numbers together and dividing by two seemed too easy. They had decided to check their answer by plugging in a hypothetical distance. They had used 20 miles as the length of the hill and figured that it took one hour to get up and 20 minutes to get down. Since the total distance traveled was 40 miles and it had taken $1^1/3$ hours to complete the trip, they had divided the former by the latter and determined that the average miles per hour traveled was 30. The group was puzzled by their answer and didn't know which was correct, 40 mph or 30 mph. I asked them whether it mattered if they used another hypothetical number besides 20 miles for the hill. They weren't sure, so I left them as they began to try 10 miles.

After listening a bit more and giving the class sufficient time to work on the problem, I pulled the groups together and asked for their answers. Three groups believed the answer to be 30 mph; seven groups believed 40 mph was the answer. Without acknowledging which answer was correct, I asked for volunteers to explain their reasoning. Peter confidently raised his hand and explained the following, "If you make two trips, up and down, each trip is equal in terms of distance. Therefore you simply add your speeds together and divide by two. The answer is 40 mph."

I asked if there were comments or questions for Peter. Susan raised her hand, saying, "I don't think you can give equal weight to the two parts—"

"And what are the parts?" I interrupted.

"The trips," she said. "Their duration is different, so they can't be given equal weight, even though I do agree the distances are equal."

"And so are you arguing for 30 mph?" I asked.

"I'm not sure," replied Susan coyly with a smile, "but I think so." I asked her to explain. "Well, our group was pretty sure 40 mph was wrong because you can't weight the trips equally, but we couldn't figure out how to weight them equally. We finally decided just to try some distances arbitrarily and see what we got. First we tried 20 miles and got 30 mph. Then we tried 10 miles and still got 30 mph. So, I guess what I'm saying is that I'm pretty sure 40 mph is wrong and I *think* 30 mph is right. But, I'm not sure why."

Claire, a senior honors student, was obviously in disagreement. I nodded to her to jump into the discussion.

"No, I disagree with your group, Susan," said Claire. "Your group has found the rate of speed traveled but not the average speed. You used the formula, rate equals distance divided by time. To find the *average* speed, you have to add the two speeds together and divide by two."

Realizing that Claire needed to reflect on what she had just said, I asked, "Is there a difference between average speed and rate?"

"Yes, the formulas are very different . . . well, actually . . . I don't know. I guess rate means the average speed traveled during a specified time period." Claire was obviously experiencing cognitive conflict.

Turning the discussion to the focus of Claire's puzzlement, I addressed the question to the class, "What is rate? Is there a difference between rate and average speed?" Because I believed my students would be more apt to use wait time if they had concretely experienced the need for it, after posing the question, I explained that, according to Rowe (1986) most teachers wait one second before calling on someone to respond and then wait only one second after that response before asking another question. There were gasps of amazement and embarrassment at the realization. I explained I would be giving them lots of wait time, then repeated the question about rate and asked them to signal me when they had had enough time. Out of the corner of my eye, I became aware of Susan. She was beginning to show a glimmer of satisfaction. After making sure that the students had all had enough time to think about the question, I smiled at Susan and she exploded in excitement. "Oh, I'm sure now. It *is* 30 mph! Rate is the same as average speed, in a sense, because if you travel a distance, X, and it takes one hour, when you divide the number of miles by 60 seconds, you're actually averaging to see how much distance you traveled each second." Several heads nodded in agreement.

To check if the class had understood Susan's reasoning, I asked for someone to volunteer to paraphrase Susan's argument and then let the discussion continue a bit more. Since consensus seemed to be reached, I asked the class for a showing of hands as to how many thought the answer was 40 mph. Seven hands went up. Twenty-one hands went up when I asked about 30 mph. Twelve were undecided and perplexed. To heighten the debate, I asked if someone believing the answer was 40 mph would be willing to try to convince the rest of the class of their answer. Meg volunteered.

"Rate is already given," she explained. "Since the rates are already figured at 20 mph and 60 mph, you simply have to add them and divide the answer by two. When you average, you divide by the number of parts you are given. In this problem that is two."

Peter raised his hand. "I thought that at first, too, Meg. But if you had a 92 on a mid-term, a 95 on the final, and a 72 on a quiz that was weighted only 25 percent of an exam, would you want the teacher to add the three scores together and divide by three?" Meg agreed she wouldn't. Peter went on, "The rates *are* figured, and the distances *are* constant, but the times aren't, so you can't give them equal weight. When you average, you divide in order to partition the whole into equal parts. In this problem, if you pretend the distance is 20 miles, as Susan's group did, then the whole distance is 40 miles and the time is $1^{1}/_3$ hours. When you divide 40 by four-thirds, you are partitioning the number of miles into groups of one-third. Every one-third of an hour, you would travel 10 miles. That translates to 30 mph." A few more heads nodded in understanding and agreement.

At this point I interrupted the thinking, saying, "Let's stop the discussion on the problem now and turn to a discussion of the learning process you just went through."

"But aren't you going to tell us the answer?" a student called out in exasperation. The class laughed in support and acknowledgment of the student.

Smiling, I said, "No. If I told you the answer, those of you still thinking about the problem would probably stop. Those of you who are sure of the answer know it with a 'logical necessity' and don't need me to confirm it. And those of you who are indeed erroneous in your reasoning, but are convinced you're right, will simply accept my answer but not change your reasoning. The answer is not half as important as the reasoning. All of you were 'taught' about averaging before, but your teachers 'told' you and 'showed' you how to do problems. You memorized their strategies. Instead, I want you to *think* in this class, to question. If I send you home tonight still thinking, I will have done my job as a teacher." I then resumed my attempt to change the focus to learning and asked how many had felt cognitive conflict during the class.

Peter raised his hand and stated emphatically with a smile, "Well, I certainly did!" The class joined him in laughter. When the laughter had subsided, he went on, "I was sure the way to find the average was to add the rates together and divide by two. Then when Susan plugged in 20 miles to find the rate and got 30 mph, her reasoning seemed right, too! I knew both answers couldn't be right, and I had two schemes that were contradictory but seemed logical. I was puzzled for a long time, trying to resolve this contradiction. Then when you asked us about rate and average speed, I began to realize that average speed was a case of finding the rate. When I came to understand that the averaging formula worked only when the parts were equally weighted and that, in this case, with these rates, they weren't, then the contradiction was resolved. I have a whole new understanding of averaging now!" Others in the class nodded in agreement.

Taking advantage of this explanation, I went on to discuss Piaget's model of equilibration in relation to Peter's comments. I defined assimilation as the way in which Peter had originally transformed and organized the problem to fit his averaging scheme; then I defined accommodation as the new understanding of averaging that Peter had constructed. The class then went on to discuss the value of cognitive conflict and the role I had played in facilitating it by using probing questions.

As class came to a close, I explained that the next several sessions would be spent observing children of different ages, in order to understand the learning process. I suggested the processes of assimilation and accommodation might be looked for during the observations, to see if equilibration was explanatory of children's learning as well.

Self-Regulation

To engage my students in constructing the concept of self-regulation, I brought several video segments to class and began the session by showing a clip of a three-month-old baby engaged in a face-to-face interaction with his mother. The class analyzed the behaviors of the mother and baby and discussed the active nature of the baby's role in eliciting a conversation with the mother. Several members of the class commented on the natural, self-regulatory manner in which the baby seemed to be learning about communication. I asked what they meant.

"Well, it's like they are taking turns in the conversation, even though it is only babble," offered Peter, "and the baby seems to be the one in charge. The mother is following *his* lead. There was one point on the clip where the mother seemed to be aggressively trying to get him to smile by bombarding him with her conversation. When that didn't work, she even resorted to tickling him. He just arched his back and turned away. When she stopped, he eventually turned back toward her and engaged her again in conversation! *He* regulated it!"

"You know, Peter," began Meg, "I was thinking as you were talking about how this child seems to be learning the rudiments of language naturalistically, and I was comparing this process to the way in which most of us probably learned to read and write language. We were drilled and reinforced about sounds of letters, often in isolation from the words. Rather than learning to read and write from *our* meaning base, the teacher was in charge. So many of my friends hated reading. They thought of it as reading to answer comprehension questions or to complete workbook pages. Maybe they were responding just like the baby, turning away in order to regulate the stimulation."

"That's an interesting reflection, Meg," I responded. "Are you suggesting that the reading process might be taught more naturalistically?"

"Yes. I don't know how yet, but it seems like learning to speak must be like learning to read. The mother in that video clip is not sitting there going, 'bbbbb . . . aaa . . . lll,' then showing the baby a ball. What she is doing seems more holistic, real, and meaningful."

"I agree, Meg," I said, "and I hope you'll continue to research that question, both while you're in school as well as when you are teaching." I then refocused the discussion by playing a second video clip of the same baby playing with a rattle. I instructed the class, "I want you to look specifically for the schemes the baby has at his disposal to explore this rattle, and whether or not you see any conflict."

After the class had viewed a section of the tape, Joanne ventured, "Well, he seems to be able to grasp the rattle when it is placed in his hand. See . . . when his mother gives him the rattle, his thumb and fingers curl around it. Does that mean he has a scheme of grasping? I guess I'm not sure what you mean by 'scheme.'"

"So that we're all using the term similarly, let's just define scheme as an 'organized pattern of behavior,'" I responded. "What do the rest of you think? Do you agree with Joanne? Does the baby seem to have a scheme of grasping?"

The class nodded in agreement. Sarah, a somewhat shy student, raised her hand and said, "Well, if a scheme is any organized pattern of behavior, then there's also lots others. I mean, we know he can arch, smile, and babble, from the clip before, and I assume he can suck."

"Right, and he can orient or look at an object," added Claire. "And you know," she continued slowly, "I think I see the conflict. He wants that rattle in his mouth. Look at his mouth. He is almost sucking. He wants to get the rattle, but he can't figure out how to reach for it."

The baby was indeed waving his arms spasmodically. When the rattle was put in his hand, he could grasp it, but he did not seem able to reach in a coordinated fashion for the rattle and bring it to his mouth. Instead, his arms flailed and his mouth began to suck.

"Yes, I agree with you, Claire," acknowledged Steven. "And you know what is interesting. Look at him, how intent he is. He's not frustrated at all. Instead, he is totally involved in trying to coordinate his grasp by reaching to where he is looking. I thought babies had short attention spans and cried when they didn't get what they wanted!"

"And are you changing your mind now about attention span?" I asked.

"Well, I'm really surprised at how long he has been involved," replied Steven.

"Do you see a difference with this task than what usually happens in school?" I probed.

"I think the main difference," replied Steven, "is that coordinating his grasping with looking and sucking is *his* goal, his question. In school, kids are usually asked to answer the teacher's questions, to complete the teacher's goals. I think there is a connection here somewhere with the point that Meg raised earlier. Teachers need to capitalize on the natural, self-regulating learning behavior of the child."

INVESTIGATIONS AND REFLECTIONS ON LEARNING

The next several classes continued in a similar fashion, with me working with children, probing for their understanding on various tasks, such as conservation of number and volume, balancing weights on a fulcrum, and displacement of volume. In each case, the class actively analyzed the children's understanding, as well as my questions. They made hypotheses about developmental differences and the structure of children's logic. In effect, the students themselves became the developmental psychologists, the epistemologists.

Teachers As Developmental Psychologists

I requested that students begin interviewing schoolchildren on various topics, in order to assess children's understanding as well as to develop their own skills at interviewing. I asked students who were already teaching to find opportunities to interview on a topic they felt they had just taught well. One of the most powerful ways to undo old schemes about teaching is to have teachers confront what children have actually learned in a unit they feel they have taught well. The process of "covering material" can be enticingly deceptive, especially when one feels it has been covered well. Probing into how children assimilated the unit (as Jessica's teacher did in Chapter 1) provides a potent contradiction to such deception. The interviews were taped so that I could give individual feedback to each student in relation to his or her probing techniques. Some interviews were also played in class and discussed. One session in particular stands out as a classic example.

Anne, a student particularly interested in early childhood education, interviewed a five-year-old boy named Johnny. Johnny's kindergarten teacher had just completed a unit on evaporation and condensation. Her kindergarteners had placed glasses of water on the windowsill and checked the water level of the glasses every morning, measuring the amount remaining. The teacher had explained that the water was evaporating "up to the clouds" and would then come down as rain. Anne decided this would be a good topic to interview Johnny on, since she was interested in Johnny's understanding of what the teacher had explained.

Anne began by asking Johnny to explain what he knew about evaporation. Johnny replied that evaporation was how we got our rain. Water from puddles and lakes "vaprates" up to the clouds. Then it came down as rain. He went on to describe to Anne the "spearment" the class had done with the glasses of water. Anne commented on how interesting all that was and probed a bit deeper, asking, "How does all that happen? How does the water get to the clouds?"

Johnny was quiet for a few minutes, obviously thinking, and then responded very seriously, "I think there must be a rain bag lady sitting up there on the clouds. She catches the water when it comes up, fills her bag, and then pours it down on the earth."

Although Anne was astounded by Johnny's reply, she went on, "How does the water get up to the rain bag lady?"

"She has a big magnet to pull the raindrops up," retorted Johnny.

When I first played the interview in class, most of the students chuckled at the "cuteness" of Johnny's replies. Some thought Johnny was just being imaginative and fantastical in fabricating an explanation. But Anne was adamant in her depiction of the interview: "I think he was really puzzled," she claimed. "He may not *really* have believed a rain bag lady sat on the clouds with a big magnet, but such an explanation made sense to him. I think he believed it was entirely possible."

Jane, another early childhood education student, had been quietly pondering Anne's interview. "You know," she offered, "I think there is some similarity in the logic of Johnny's explanation and that of the child I interviewed."

I asked her to explain.

"Well," she went on, "I interviewed one of my kindergarten children on how the leaves change colors in the fall. We had just completed a unit on autumn. We had collected autumn leaves for art projects, had done rubbings to show the "veins," and I had even demonstrated with celery and food coloring how nourishment travels to all parts of the plant. I thought I had done a good job with the unit, but this child told me that the green leaves fall off the tree and then the colored ones come on! When I asked her if she had ever seen a lot of green leaves lying around on the ground, she said that they must have gone underground. I pushed her by asking if I would see them if we dug a hole together. She seemed bored by my question and commented simply that we would come to the devil first!"

At this point, the class dissolved into laughter. When it had subsided, Jane explained, "I thought she was pulling my leg, but now I see a connection with the way in which Johnny was thinking. Both Anne's and my topics required the child to understand the transformation process of molecular change. Obviously this concept requires abstractions way beyond the ability of five-year-olds."

David, a 32-year-old Englishman who had spent 10 years working with adolescents in Outward Bound programs, interrupted her. "We seem to be inferring that abstractions are too difficult for five-year-olds because of their age. I interviewed a seventh grader and found that at a certain point he had trouble with abstractions as well. I was questioning him about the tides, since I knew his class had just completed a study of marine biology. There was much he *was* clear about; for example, he told me that tidal changes are caused by the gravitational pull of the moon, and that the change occurs every six hours. He even went so far as to point out that England was having high tide when New England was having low tide. But, when I asked him how the water got from England to New England in six hours, he was puzzled, showing that he didn't really understand the movement of the moon, nor its effect. Well, actually, he did offer an explanation — a tidal wave, which he claimed he had never seen, but he stated that he wouldn't want to be on an island in the middle of the ocean when the tide was changing!"

The class once again broke into laughter. I interrupted by asking, "David, you and Jane are using the word *abstraction*. Can either of you explain to us what you mean by it?"

"Sure, I can explain what *I* mean, anyway," Jane replied. "Understanding molecular change requires making inferences about processes that explain a change that is not immediately visible. It's not concrete to children. They can see that water has indeed disappeared, but they can't 'see' *how* it disappears. I wonder if they even understand change at all."

"That seems like a leap. Why do you say that?" asked Peter.

"Well, because any change requires making inferences about the connections between the states. Do they make those connections? I don't know," Jane responded.

"I think Johnny was thinking about causality," offered Anne. "He tried to explain how the drops got up to the clouds — "

"But maybe that is because *you* asked him for an explanation," Jane interrupted. "It may not have been anything he particularly had wondered about."

Steven chimed in, supporting Jane's point: "You know, viewed from that perspective, the responses of the two children now seem very logical. If their logic is not abstract, and they don't really understand transformations or causality, even in a concrete way, then their explanations make a lot of sense."

"You lost me, Steven," commented Meg, shaking her head. Several students nodded in agreement.

Steven went on: "Johnny has probably seen how magnets work; he may even have played with them himself. He made a connection between what he knew had a causal relationship (magnets pick up filings) and what he couldn't explain (how raindrops got up to the clouds). Isn't that what we all did originally with the average-speed problem — used what we did know about figuring averages to solve the problem? A mathematician would probably have thought our original approach to the average-speed problem was illogical. To us, it made perfect sense."

Several heads nodded in acknowledgment of Steven's interpretation.

"You know," Jane began slowly, "I'm just beginning to understand how important it is to understand how the learners you are working with think. As a teacher, you almost have to be able to get inside the child's head, to think like that child."

Susan nodded in agreement and extended Jane's point. "I was also thinking that it seems like learning is a case of going from the known to the unknown. *What* one knows, and *how* one knows affect what one can learn. If the teacher helps the child make connections, then the knowledge becomes a connected network of meaning and relations. Otherwise, knowledge might be just separate bits and facts to be memorized."

"And then probably forgotten," added Steven in agreement.

Teachers As Epistemologists

I've often thought that one of the problems with present education-al institutions is that they encourage the idea that learning actually ends. Young learners are taught to believe that, when they finish a work sheet, they are done learning, and that idea is reinforced all through schooling. Workbook finished? Good; done! Posttest successfully completed? Good; on to the next unit. Degree completed? Great; done! Little integration exists with learning outside the classroom. Instead of learning being viewed as a continuous process of inquiry and investigation, it is assessed as a "measurable" accumulation of discrete bits of knowledge.

In looking at my own practice, I realized that I had always given an exam as a way to evaluate whether my students had learned or not, yet I was coming to see this procedure (even though it was a take-home exam) as being in direct contradiction to the principles I had been advocating. I wanted instead to capitalize on the *process* of learning, rather than evaluation of the *product*; I wanted to maximize the opportunity to probe my students' understanding in a way that would cause them to continue questioning, rather than to accept rote answers. In particular, I wanted students to leave my class with a desire and thirst for continued inquiry. I wanted to eradicate misconceptions that learning only takes place in a classroom while teachers explain what *they* know.

I thus decided to offer my students a choice between (1) a class period where I would use a modified form of a clinical interview, using open-ended questions to probe their understanding of Piaget's theory or (2) a take-home exam. They unanimously opted for the former choice. I gave them a list of questions that I wanted them to research and be prepared to discuss in class, and I videotaped the class session as documentation of learning. Excerpts from the transcript follow.

"Let's start by grappling with the notion of equilibration," I began. "Would someone like to explain it and give us an example?"

Sarah ventured, "Well, it seems like a whole process of how you learn and obtain knowledge. You reach a higher level of understanding by having conflicts, a challenge to your initial way of understanding, and then you resolve it."

I checked for class understanding of Sarah's description by asking for someone to paraphrase Sarah's depiction. I then asked if anyone disagreed with Sarah or wanted to add to the explanation.

"First you assimilate your environment by taking it in," offered John. "This presents confusion to you, and because you want to feel secure you resolve the confusion. The process is equilibration. Then afterward you accommodate."

"No, I disagree with you, John," responded Sarah. "The process is equilibration. You are simply seeking equilibrium. You assimilate first, then you accommodate to achieve a balance."

David was looking puzzled. "I think," he began, "of the two as going on simultaneously. Once you reach equilibrium, you don't stop there. You seek to go on because of assimilation. Assimilation and accommodation happen together. That is where the conflict comes from."

I asked David to explain further.

"You already have a scheme," he continued, "which you use to 'act on' the world. You change your experience by transforming it, organizing it, according to your logic. Piaget describes a 'reaching beyond the grasp,' and I agree with him. I think he means we need to know more; we seek novelty; we seek to extend, change, grow and accommodate. That process creates conflict."

It was obvious the class was pondering David's interpretation of equilibration. I waited a bit, then asked Sarah if she wanted to respond.

She said, hesitatingly, "I agree that we each have frames of existence. But something has to enter that frame that causes you to question, like something you think you know, and then new information which doesn't fit. So, you try and resolve it by either ignoring it or by incorporating it into a new frame. That's accommodation."

Claire entered the conversation. "I do believe conflict has to be there before equilibration is over, but, how does the conflict come? That is the question. I think it is part of equilibration, but aren't there some things you learn without conflict? Don't you sometimes just assimilate or accommodate without having a conflict?"

Mumblings and dissention began. It was obvious that most class members were confused. David raised his hand, and I nodded to him to go on.

"I'm going to add more confusion, because I want to go back and revise a bit of what I said earlier. I wouldn't have seen it this way unless I had heard all this conflict (laughter from the class). Now I see that assimilation and accommodation go on all through life. You can have conflict, but you can also just accommodate, like when you imitate. That's an accommodation with no assimilation. Maybe you can also assimilate without any accommodation, I'm not sure. But, I think more important, you can't break them apart and say this (assimilation) is happening now and then conflict, then accommodation, because you will lose sight of the whole picture. Both processes go on throughout life."

"I need us to get concrete," Joanne demanded. "I need examples. When I was doing the research for equilibration, the way I organized it in my mind was to go back to the average-speed problem we did in class the first night. Assimilation was what I did when I first approached the problem. I made it into a simple situation of add the parts and then divide by the number of parts. A conflict began for me when others began talking about how they divided the distance by the time it took, because both schemes were logical to me, but they were contradictory. First I ignored the conflict. I was convinced the answer was 40 mph because I believed that the way to find an average was to add the parts up and then divide by the number of parts, and I didn't want to let go of my scheme. Later, when I went home, the contradiction was still there. I puzzled about it for a long time at home. Eventually I accommodated when I developed a new understanding of average speed. So, I think I went through the whole process."

I asked for a paraphrase or extension, and Peter explained, "Equilibration is the finding out that a contradiction exists to your original scheme, or that it doesn't work for a specific situation. This situation creates an internal conflict which is resolved by an accommodation, the development of a higher-level understanding."

"If you had asked us to do an averaging problem without the variable of speed, like scores, our assimilatory scheme would have worked. So we wouldn't have had any conflict." Joanne directed her point at me.

"True. Would you have learned anything?" I queried.

Several students responded at once. "No, we simply would have been practicing — how boring."

"But that's what most schools do," Meg pointed out. "Teachers show children how to compute, and then the children practice how the teacher got the answer, year after year."

I waited a bit for the importance of Meg's comment to be acknowledged, and then began to probe. "We've been saying that the learners, in assimilating, try to match what they know to each new situation. There are learning theorists who say that learning is a case of making associations, and that when associations are reinforced new knowledge is developed. Would you classify Piaget as an associationist?"

"No," ventured Joanne. "I think they are almost opposites, because Piaget emphasizes contradiction. When our old schemes about average didn't work, then we began learning. It was because the association *didn't* work."

David agreed and added, "Yes, I also think that, according to Piaget, the learner is more active—"

I interrupted David and asked him to explain what he meant by "active."

"Mentally active," he continued. "The learner seems to seek the mismatch, in order to test theories, not just passively make associations and have them reinforced. We *act on* our environment."

"Yes, like when we classify or order things; we are acting on our environment," added Claire.

Betsy, an older student who had been a teacher's aide for years and was returning to school for certification, was obviously reflecting. She began to share her thoughts. "I think from all this I'm learning how important it is for the teacher to facilitate that activity, too. I'll never forget that first night of class, the interaction that went on between all of us. It was powerful, and that doesn't happen with workbooks and dittos. Experience is so important."

I acknowledged Betsy's comment, but probed further. "Let's dig at that word, *experience*. Both Locke and Montessori discussed the need for experience, of learning with the senses. What kind of experience is Piaget talking about?"

Claire answered tentatively, "I think he means physical experience, that we learn from our actions."

"Is *all* physical experience constructive?" I challenged. "Can we differentiate between that which is constructive and that which is not?"

"I think constructive experience relates to figuring things out on your own," offered Peter. "You don't just do what you're told to do. Instead, you make inferences and investigate connections. If *you* figure it out, it stays with you."

Betsy, who had remained quiet at first, now seemed eager to share. "Seems like a constructive experience," she began, "might have cognitive conflict and self-regulation in it. For example, one day I was working with a group of fifth graders. We were using base-10 blocks and multiplying with numbers that ended in zero. All the kids went through the same actions, but one girl in particular was really puzzled. She did several problems. In fact, she worked for about 40 minutes and then, with excitement and satisfaction, she explained to me why when you multiply with a number that ends in zero, the answer will have a zero. She had had a *constructive* experience. The others simply physically manipulated the materials. She had hypothesized, investigated, and explained to herself *why* the pattern occurred. I think equilibration brings about *real* understanding. Other experiences can bring about understanding but usually only a shaky one, which can be knocked over with a stick. Hers from this experience was solid."

"Betsy, it sounds as if you're making a distinction between success and understanding," I proffered.

"Yes, yes!" she responded. "I think when I was a child in school, my teachers only looked at success — whether I could get answers correctly or not. They never looked at *real* understanding. Think how powerful education might be if we, as teachers, really worked toward children's understanding."

The importance of Betsy's reflection was felt by the class, and quiet ensued for a few minutes. Eventually, John began, "You know, I came in here tonight thinking I understood equilibration, cognitive conflict, constructive experience, et cetera. After this discussion, I feel I have a much deeper understanding of the concepts, but I'm still a little unsure and a part of me wants to write the definitions down and have them checked. How do I know if I've learned?"

"Do you think you would have learned more if you'd come in here tonight and taken a test?" Meg asked.

"No," responded John. "It's just that I've never learned this way before, and that's why I'm saying, how do I know if I've learned?"

"What *is* learning?" I probed. The class was quiet, even after a long wait time. "What is learning?" I asked again. "Is it the accumulation of answers?"

"That's part of it," several members responded.

"Is it sufficient?" I asked.

"No," most responded in unison.

"Is it necessary?" The class was quiet again. "Let's take the case of the average-speed problem," I began. "Some of you left here the first night of class still puzzled. Joanne, you said that you weren't sure when you left class how to do it, but you went home thinking about 'average speed' and what it meant. When you began the problem, you were convinced the strategy of adding the two together and dividing by two would work. Even though you went home not knowing the answer, do you think you learned anything?"

After much thought, Joanne responded, "Yes, I guess I did, because first I had to go through the puzzlement and questioning of my old schemes before I could construct a new scheme, at least if we're talking about *real* understanding. You could have told us which way was right, but I doubt my understanding would have changed. I just would have said that you add parts and divide by the number of parts when you have one kind of problem. When it is a speed problem, you find the rate. I might have been successful at problems, but my understanding wouldn't have been as solid as that which Betsy was describing. I wouldn't have understood the connection between the problems. They would have been separate problems with separate formulas."

I nodded in agreement. "I will share with you," I explained, "that as a teacher I am constantly monitoring your progress and making decisions about your needs. At times I let you struggle because the concepts are difficult and the struggle is important to your understanding. At other times, when a simple fact or a label is to be learned, it is far more expedient for me to tell you than for you to discover. Such teacher decision making is so important. I could kill inquiry by telling too much too soon, or, reciprocally, by letting you flounder in confusion too long. As a teacher I try to maintain a clear sense of my objectives. I take responsibility for not letting you go too far astray with erroneous ideas, but, on the other hand, there are times when confusion and cognitive conflict are a step above a clear but obvious misunderstanding. I have to make that judgment. I evaluate your learning by looking at your thought process. I also don't assume that learning only happens in this classroom. I want to empower you, to make you independent, autonomous learners. I want you to continue to inquire. If scientists accepted known facts as truths, science might never advance. Einstein once said that his most important trait as a scientist was his imagination, meaning that he questioned; he wondered 'why,' and 'what if.'"

On that note, the course came to a close, but students left with much on their minds and many questions.

Greener Still: Investigations in Language

*The writer's evolving text exposes the writer to the writer,
the writer seeing, the writer thinking. The student who was
living one life becomes a writer and lives twice, thrice, a
multiplication of lives, each life of words reassembling the
lived life into new meanings.*

— Murray, "What Happens When
Students Learn to Write"

English is a complicated but interesting language. Because of its diverse
roots it is not consistently phonetic, a fact that has led many linguists to
advocate spelling reform and many teachers to throw up their arms in
despair and resort to memorization and drill. The playwright George
Bernard Shaw once quipped in fact that "in English the word *fish* might
as well be spelled *ghoti* . . . *gh* as in *rough*, *o* as in *women*, and *ti* as in
vacation" (in Henderson, 1985, p. 6).

Although a phonetic analysis results in many inconsistencies, when
a four-tiered investigation organized by knowledge of phonetics, patterns, meaning, and etymology is used, much more order and logical
consistency are observed. For example, *fish* would never be spelled with
gh since *ough* is a pattern, as is *tion*. The silent *g* in *sign* may be
confusing until one relates it to the word *signal*; *Robert* is spelled with
one *b* because it was originally French and pronounced "Rō/bèrt."

Young learners may spell *fish* as *fs* or even *fes*, yet their spellings
have more logical sense than Shaw's example and are representative of
the beginning formulation of rules that govern language (Henderson,
1985). While good spellers may have memorized many words, that process was made far easier by the use of rules. Unfortunately, these rules
are often only accessible on a tacit level. Teachers rarely help make them
explicit because they themselves were not taught to investigate the

language for consistency, and because the phonetic disorder is far more obvious and serves as a deterrent. As Henderson (1985) notes, however, teachers who have such a thorough understanding of the rules of English "will be more likely to inspire children to examine words with interest and care" (p. 8).

Writing instruction in the schools has fared a little better than spelling. The recent move toward focusing on process rather than product has brought with it an emphasis on revision and drafts, as well as learner-centered investigations into authors' styles. Although these changes are positive, they are often threatening to teachers, since they rarely perceive themselves as writers and therefore are at a loss as to how to encourage the process.

A case was made in Chapter 2 for involving teachers, as learners, in investigations in content areas, followed by reflection on their learning process, in order to enable the construction of pedagogical principles. This chapter documents my attempt over the last several years to do so in the field of language arts.

TEACHERS AS LEARNERS: INQUIRY AND INVENTION IN SPELLING

Class began with an investigation centered around the following list of words:

remissible	extensible
catchable	endurable
playable	edible
admirable	indispensable
admissible	kissable
permissible	passable
plausible	penetrable
potable	visible
changeable	fixable
guidable	incredible
explosible	divisible
amenable	readable
available	

After dividing the students into groups of four participants each, I asked them to join me in a linguistic investigation, first sorting the words by the spelling of the suffixes, and then looking for patterns and rules that might be advanced to explain when to use -ible and when to use -able.

The groups worked for approximately a half hour, discussing among themselves various patterns and possible rules that might explain the pattern; then I convened a "general assembly" and asked the "linguistic research groups" to share their findings.

Pam, serving as spokesperson for her group, began by tacking on the board two large sheets of paper with the following lists of words:

catchable	plausible
playable	remissible
admirable	admissible
potable	permissible
changeable	explosible
guidable	divisible
amenable	incredible
available	visible
endurable	extensible
penetrable	edible
kissable	
readable	
indispensable	
passable	
fixable	

"Our group believes," she proposed, "that if the root word is a whole word then you add *-able*; if the root word is substantially changed, you add *-ible*."

"Questions or comments from other groups?" I countered, to invite a discussion.

A second student, Hannah, disagreed. "Our group thought that at first, too," she acknowledged. "But when Cathy came by, she drew our attention to several words that violated our rule. I would like to do that with you, if I may. How do you explain *amenable, flexible, potable*, and *penetrable?*" she asked.

Pam was undaunted. "Well, we figured that *penetrable* was too long to say and so the *ate* had been taken out, and we hoped the root word of *amenable* was *amen*, Latin for 'so be it'." The class laughed good-naturedly at her humor.

"Did anyone look up the root word of *amenable?*" I interjected.

"We did," said David, responding for his group. "It comes from the French *amener*, which means 'to lead up.' We also looked up *potable* and found that the word was derived from the French *potare*. Our group wondered if *potable* and *amenable* were spelled with *-able* because they are French words."

"Look up *penetrable*," Pam requested.

David obliged and subsequently reported, with disappointment, that *penetrable* stemmed from the Latin verb *penetrare*. Both rules were now under question, and Sarah, a fluent French speaker, added further evidence to disprove David's rule. "Even if *penetrable* were French," she offered, "that wouldn't prove anything. The French use both endings, *-ible* and *-able*, too; for example, *divisible* is French. And I have further questions for Pam," Sarah continued. "Are you assuming that changing a *y* to *i*, like in *variable*, is not changing the root word? And what about the words *flexible* and *sensible*?" (drawing in a couple of words not in the original list). "According to your rule, they should be spelled with *-able*." Obviously perplexed, she mused, "The deeper question seems to be why both languages use the same suffixes and how they decided which to use."

"Right—more problems," Pam acknowledged. "We also couldn't explain *hospitable*. Shouldn't it be *hospitaliable*?"

"What is the root of *hospitable*?" I asked.

Pam looked it up in the dictionary and found to her surprise that the root was *hospit* (French) and it therefore fit her rule.

At this point I wanted to expand the discussion to look at other possible rules. "Pam, let's underline the words that your rule had trouble explaining," I suggested, "and let's hear from some other groups." Pam underlined *amenable, potable, penetrable, flexible*, and *sensible*, and then I asked, "Does any group have a rule that either explains the exceptions to Pam's rule, or is perhaps a totally different rule?"

Karen, a second-grade teacher, offered to serve as spokesperson for her group. "We noticed a connection between the *-ible* words," she began. "It seems that *-ion* could also be added as a suffix to the root, for example *division, extension, remission, admission, vision*—"

"We noticed that, too," Hannah interrupted her. "But, we couldn't figure out what to do with *edible*. Maybe your group had success?"

"No, that was a problem for us, too," Karen admitted. "We simply decided that the English language has strange exceptions."

"Perhaps it's French," David offered with a smile. He looked it up and reported that it was Late Latin in origin, from the root *edibilis*. *Edible* didn't fit any of the rules offered so far. And two other exceptions, *sensible* and *incredible*, were subsequently added.

"All right, so we still have several exceptions," I summarized. "Any ideas?"

"I think our rule might help," said Meg, speaking for a group as yet unheard from. "We decided that, if a root word ends in *d* or *s*, you add *-ible*; otherwise, add *-able*. Unless the root word is a word in itself, then you add *-able* automatically."

We checked out each of the words on the list. *Passable, readable,* and *kissable* could be explained by the second half of the rule, whereas *edible, sensible,* and *incredible* could be explained by the first half. Meg's rule held great promise until we came to *flexible* and *fixable.* They both ended in *x,* and both *flex* and *fix* could stand alone. According to Meg's rule, *flexible* should end with *-able.* After some discussion, a second exception was found. According to Meg's rule, *terrible* should also end with *-able.* A few groans were heard as these exceptions were found.

'Is there a *real* rule?" Pam asked, jokingly, but with some disbelief in her voice. The class joined her in laughter.

"That's an important question, Pam," I responded seriously. "We might conclude that there isn't. But two questions loom in my mind. First, how do we know that we have tried enough possibilities to conclude that there is no rule? Secondly, I would like to probe into what you mean by 'real.'"

"Well, I guess I mean that some famous linguist somewhere has proven a rule—that there is a fact, a truth, that explains when to use *-able* and *-ible*," Pam responded.

"May I play the devil's advocate with you?" I asked. Pam consented, so I continued, "I'd like to be philosophical for a minute and propose, for the sake of discussion, that knowledge is simply a case of human invention. What I mean is that humans construct schemes that make sense of their experiences. Contradictions arise from investigations and experimentation and from social interactions. Truth, therefore, is temporary, since it depends on social consensus and experimentation; it's truth only as long as it is explanatory, as long as it works. The point here is not to learn a rule that linguistics may have proposed in the past, but to construct rules that help us make sense out of the contradictions in our language, rules that will serve to foster better spelling."

Quiet ensued for a minute, then David commented, "That's nice. I like thinking about knowledge that way. It's like the justice system—innocent until proven guilty, or truth until disproven. From that perspective, knowledge becomes a case of continuous inquiry and continuous constructing."

"I think I disagree," Sarah interjected. "Are you saying that anything is true as long as you believe it is true?"

"No," I responded, "because social consensus and experimentation provide a boundary. I'm not saying all individual ideas are truths, only that all ideas can be put forth to be argued, debated, and tested. Some ideas explain more and thus stand the test of time longer. Let's look at science for a minute. During the 1800s, light was believed to be composed of waves. Thomas Young had shown convincingly that when a beam of light was projected through a razor-thin slit, narrower than the wavelength of the light, interference or diffraction occurred. This diffraction could only be explained by a wave theory. Planck proved, in contradiction to Young's theory, that light was composed of small particles (called *photons*) traveling in a similar fashion to billiard balls. When they hit an object, they knocked a particle out of the mass of that object, just as a billiard ball hitting another would send it traveling at the same speed as the original ball. His proposal explained refraction and the photoelectric effect, whereas the wave theory had been insufficient, but a paradox remained. How could light be particles, and yet be waves at the same time? Einstein eventually resolved the contradiction by proving that light was both. He proposed that light is nothing but a rapidly alternating electromagnetic field traveling through space in the form of waves. Whether we perceive light as photons or as waves depends on the observer, the question asked, and the measurement system used. Each idea was considered knowledge when it was proposed, because it was explanatory of phenomena observed. It served as 'truth' until experimentation and social consensus in the scientific community deemed otherwise."

I paused to let students reflect, then continued, "A friend of mine, who is a scientist, claims that the facts we come to believe are truth (the content) are not the real science but only the history of science. In other words, the concepts such as gravity, magnetism, or thermodynamics are simply explanations that have been advanced by scientists to explain various phenomena. If we look at them through time, they simply become the history of science. The real science, he claims, is the investigating, the inquiring, the imagining."

Sarah protested, "But isn't spelling a different case? Either there is a linguistic rule as to when to use *-ible*, or there isn't. We aren't talking about theories here."

"You raise an interesting point," I acknowledged. Then I challenged her: "What *is* spelling?"

After a long wait time, Karen offered timidly, "Isn't it just the correct juxtapositioning of letters in words?" Several students nodded in agreement.

David disagreed. "No, I don't think so," he began. "Until this course, I thought so. But now I think that perhaps it is a much deeper field. It involves investigating patterns and sounds, constructing rules, researching cultural derivations, as well as studying changes in language historically. Looking at spelling as only a skill is like calling computation or arithmetic, mathematics. It's a small part of a much bigger whole."

Charlotte, a first-grade teacher who had been fairly quiet until now, offered pensively, "It seems to me that we are discussing a dichotomy between process and content. Sarah and Karen seem concerned with content — Will I get the rule, or word, right? David is talking about a way of investigating, a way of thinking. That's process. I wonder if they are really separate, though. As I reflect back on the spelling investigation that started this discussion, I know I learned content as well as process. Although I don't know if our final rule is 'correct,' I do know that I learned to spell approximately 30 words correctly in the process and that the rule holds for most of them. And, perhaps more important, my frame of reference has been enlarged. Even if Cathy told me 'the rule' now — if there is one — I would be apt to say, Ah yes, but when we came up with our rules, we found exceptions, so let's do the same with this. I think that process is important. That's how knowledge grows; otherwise, it would be stagnant."

Sarah was obviously reflecting on Charlotte's words, but she still had doubts. "I don't know," she began, "I'm having a problem with the fact that we're all trying to come up with a rule and no one is telling us the real one. I might leave here tonight thinking that my rule is correct when it isn't. Or worse still, you might tell us the real rule, but I would probably forget it and remember mine, since I was so involved in figuring it out!" With that comment, we all joined Sarah in sympathetic laughter.

When the giggles had subsided, I suggested, "You know, Sarah, there are at least three points you raise in your comment that I think we should consider. First, it is interesting that you fear that if you don't learn 'the rule' in class you won't learn it at all. Does learning only take place in school?" I paused and then continued, "Second, you noted that you are more apt to remember something that you have figured out than that which is told to you. So why is it so important to you to have me tell you a rule? And third, how will you know it's truth if you accept it and don't investigate yourself?" I knew my questions demanded more reflection than specific answers or responses, so I waited a bit and then went on. "I will reassure you, though, that I take my role as teacher very seriously. I have considered carefully my goal in structuring the prior investigation. If I had wanted you to memorize a specific rule, I would not have bothered having you sort words and look for patterns in the first place. It would have been much more efficient simply to tell you a rule and have you practice it. My goal is much different; I want you to investigate the language, search for patterns, and research word derivations. I want you to become active explorers of language roots, rather than only technically correct spellers. As a teacher, I also take responsibility for facilitating experimentation and social interaction. I could say to you, That's an interesting rule that you've come up with, now here is the real one. But I would never do that. Instead, I try to facilitate cognitive disequilibrium. I point out exceptions that I'm aware of that cause problems for your rules, and I try to foster debates and discussion. By arguing and testing out ideas in groups, we come up with exceptions for each other to consider, and that also promotes construction."

"You did that with our group when you pointed out several words that our rule could not explain," commented Hannah.

"Yes. And I would like us to return to that investigation, if you will, because I think we left a few things unanswered. The present rule we were working with regarding *s* and *d*, and root words, held for many more words than our previous rules, but we did find exceptions that led Pam to ask if there was a *real* rule. It's a legitimate question, which I think we need to address, as a group. What information do we need to know, as fellow linguists, in order to answer her question conclusively?"

Hannah responded quickly. "I've been thinking about that," she began, "and it seems to me that we could approach the task in two different directions. Either we could explore all *-ible* and *-able* words with a systematic analysis governed by etymology, which might take a lifetime, or we could hope our rule was close, since we only had a few exceptions to explain. We could then assume there is a rule and start by analyzing the exceptions."

The class sentiment was clearly in favor of the latter approach. I decided to structure the investigation even closer. "Why don't we begin," I suggested, "by looking up the root words for the exceptions—*flexible*, *fixable*, and *terrible*—since Meg's rule requires us to know the root word. We assumed *fix* and *flex* are roots, but I'm sure we could trace those back further." This search produced the following derivations: the Latin *flexus* for *flexible*, the Middle English *terribilis* for *terrible*, and the Middle English *fixen* for *fixable*.

"The roots of *flex* and *terrible* end in *s*!" Meg declared in surprise. "Look up *edible*, *kissable*, and *passable*," she urged us. The result was the Late Latin *edibilis* for *edible*, the Middle English *kissen* for *kissable*, and the Middle English *passen* for *passable*. The class was getting excited. We decided to break down the list and give five words to each group to look up. Our results are shown in Table 4.1.

Table 4.1. Words Ending with *-able* and *-ible*, and Their Origins and Derivatives

-able words			*-ible* words		
Word	*Origin*[a]	*Derivative*	*Word*	*Origin*[a]	*Derivative*
catchable	ME	cacchen	plausible	L	plausibilis
playable	OE	plega	remissible	ME	remissus
admirable	MFr	admirer	admissible	ML	admissibilis
potable	Fr	potare	permissible	ML	permissibilis
changeable	ME	changen	explosible	Fr	explosus
guidable	Fr, OP	guida	divisible	Fr	divisus
amenable	Fr	amener	incredible	ME	incredibilis
available	ME	availen	visible	Fr, L	visibilis
endurable	ME	enduren	extensible	L	extensus
penetrable	L	penetrare	edible	L	edibilis
readable	ME	reden			
indispensable	ME	dispensen			
kissable	ME	kissen			
fixable	ME	fixen			
passable	ME	passen			

[a]Key: ME=Middle English; L=Latin; Fr=French; OP=Old Provençal; OE=Old English; MFr=Middle French; ML=Middle Latin

"Look at the consistency!" exclaimed Pam. "All the roots of the *-ible* words are similar, ending either in *-sus* or *-ibilis*. Our rule was close; we just hadn't probed far enough!"

Excitement and self-satisfaction were high, and when Sarah spoke, she obviously spoke for all. "You know," she commented reflectively, "when I studied French I found it very interesting because I was learning about the culture and the history of a people through studying the language. For the first time, tonight, I felt that same excitement for English. It was fascinating to figure out why words are spelled the way they are and to look at how they have changed over time. I would love to continue looking at how the English language has changed from early times to now."

"I'm so glad you feel that way, Sarah," I said with a smile. "Let's make that our next investigation."

INVESTIGATING THE ENGLISH LANGUAGE

I am a firm believer that teachers who have explored etymology not only have a keener appreciation and excitement for the language, but place a higher value on the process of construction. Viewing the changes and shifts in language that have occurred through time (an evolutionary perspective) provides an interesting parallel to the study of children who are learning to spell (a developmental perspective) and facilitates an appreciation for the natural, emerging patterns of spelling which children invent. Henderson's book, *Teaching Spelling* (1985), promotes a similar viewpoint and provides a history of the English language as well as samples of children's emerging spelling rules. I request that my students read his book; our discussion of it usually centers around the following historical information.

The English language is about 1,500 years old, and most linguists agree that it has gone through three distinct phases, each of which lasted approximately 500 years. These phases are commonly known as Old English (A.D. 600–1100), Middle English (A.D. 1100–1500), and Modern English (1500 to the present).

The first attempts at written English were highly phonetic and consistent. *E* represented our current long *a* sound; *i*, our current long *e* sound. *A* was used for the sound of *a* in father, whereas a short *a* was represented by *ae*. *U* symbolized the vowel sound in *moon*, and *y* was used for both short and long sounds of *i*. Not only was the written form phonetic, the language itself was synthetic, as was Latin; that is, nouns were spelled differently depending on whether they were subjects or objects and pronouns and adjectives changed for gender and plurality.

In 1066, with the Battle of Hastings, William the Conqueror brought French influence to the land, which affected both pronunciation and spelling. Several new sounds were introduced such as *oi, ou, ea*, the *ce* in *dance* and *fence*, as well as the soft *c* sound in *cinder*. Confusion reigned over whether to pronounce the *h* in words like *hospital* and *heir*, since it was pronounced in Latin but not in French. Also at this time *v* and *u* sounds were identical and when doubled produced *w*. Spelling *love* or *dove* with the phonetic *u* would have produced *lw* or *dw*, an improper combination without a vowel; hence our current spellings were born.

During the Renaissance, with the return of Latin and Greek influence, a major shift in spelling occurred, known as the Great Vowel Shift. The Old English long *a* (as in *father*) became the modern long *a* (as in *cake*), leaving the Old English long *e* with a problem, since it was pronounced like long *a* (*clean* was pronounced "clane"). Hence, long *e*

changed to long *i* (*feef* to *five*) and the principle of doubling the consonant at syllable junctures appeared, to show short versus long vowel
sounds. With the publication of Johnson's dictionary, meaning took
precedence over phonetics in order to establish and maintain etymological roots; for example, *mnemonic* is spelled with a silent *m* because of its
relationship to *amnesia* and *amnesty*.

After reading and discussing this brief history of the English language, I engage students in the task of depicting the phases and shifts in
its symbolic form. Representing knowledge in a visual art form often
produces new connections and insights in relation to the object being
represented (Fosnot, 1981; Golomb, 1974; Ives & Meringoff, 1979). One
semester, three students working together produced the representation
depicted in Figure 4.1.

Amy, serving as spokesperson for her group, explained the drawing
as follows. "We built a spiral, to represent growth and change. At the
bottom is Old English. It was highly phonetic and incorporated the
fewest number of cultural influences during the evolution of the language; therefore we represented it as a small, consistent circle and attached it to a base. As new cultural influences occurred, they provided
tugs. The circle widens to represent Middle English. Because this phase
is characterized by a focus on patterns of sounds, rather than simple
phonetics, we used the incline from the base to the second circle to
represent this qualitative shift. Further cultural tugs produced an even
wider circle of Modern English, with a shift upward characterized by
meaning, word derivations, and new patterns of syllable junctures to
clarify vowel sounds."

I asked the class if there were any comments, questions, or suggestions for Amy's group.

"Oh, Amy," David commented with awe, "I think that's a beautiful
representation, not only of the changes in language but of learning in
general. The cultural tugs that you have depicted are like social interaction; it produces tugs, too, and we shift and grow as a result. Each ring
is but a new way of viewing our world."

Our class was quiet as we contemplated David's words, and I determined it was time to begin our study of children learning to spell.

INVESTIGATING CHILDREN'S SPELLING

The research of Henderson and his students (Henderson, 1981,
1985; Henderson & Beers, 1980) documents five stages that learners go
through as they develop spelling knowledge. Stage 1 is typical of the

Figure 4.1. Symbolic representation of evolutionary changes in language.

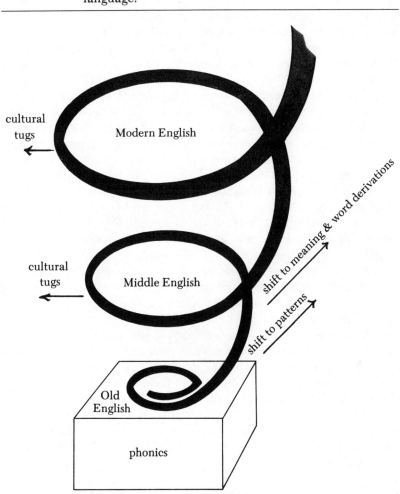

young preschooler who has little understanding of what a word is. Asked to find where it says "my mommy" in the sentence, "My mommy went to the store to buy ice cream," she may point to one word because "my mommy" is based on one object, or she may run her finger across the whole sentence, or she may write "my mommy" with the symbols 122AD. She does not yet understand that letters have sounds and that words are made up of letters.

Stage 2 (often observed in kindergarteners) is characterized, in contrast, by direct sound-to-letter matches. Glenda Bissex (1980) provides a classic example of this stage. Her son, after failing repeatedly to get her attention while she was studying, wrote the following message: "R U DF" (Are you deaf?). Children at this stage are beginning to decode, but usually only by representing the most prominent consonant sounds.

Children begin to add some vowels by stage 3 (typically observed in first and second graders), but still with a direct sound-to-letter match. Short vowel sounds are matched to the letter name that sounds the closest; for example *rain* may be misspelled "ran," whereas *sit* is frequently misspelled "set" because the short *i* sound is similar to the name of the letter *e*. Interestingly, many of the substitutions by children found at this stage are similar to Old English spellings.

Stage 4 children (ages 7–12) are beginning to consider patterns as sounds. *Car* begins to be spelled correctly, including the *a*, instead of just *cr*. The *ai* appears in *rain*, and short vowel sounds begin to be used as well as long vowel sounds with markers such as the silent *e*. Patterns usually missed are those where meaning is important, such as in the word *sign* (commonly misspelled "sine"), or where suffixes such as *-ed*, *-es*, or *-ing* are added. Many of the patterns that do appear at this stage parallel the patterns that appeared in Middle English.

Stage 5 (ages 10–18) is characterized by analysis of words for their derivatives and meaning, hence suffixes are usually added properly and syllable junctures show the doubling principle. In the sense that a beginning etymological analysis is apparent, it is closely akin to the shift from Middle English to Modern English.

Although Henderson (1985) describes well the development of the naturalistic spelling of children and illustrates the stages with examples, it is a far more potent experience for teachers to collect and analyze their own children's work together. My classes at SCSU usually contain teachers from the preschool level through Grade 8. At times, a secondary teacher or two are squeezed in. I request that each student collect samples of children's work, which we then analyze in class in relation to the framework provided by Henderson. The expressed purpose is not to match children to stages, but to analyze the misspellings for rules children may be using in their attempts to put words into print. In other words, we try to give meaning to their actions. The developmental research simply serves as a possible framework in our investigations. As teachers gain the ability to analyze children's errors as representative of logical, rule-governed schemes, rather than simply as mistakes to be corrected, they gain respect for learners and develop a clearer sense of how to facilitate growth and understanding.

TEACHERS AS AUTHORS: WRITING AS PROCESS

Perhaps one of the major reasons I first became a teacher is that I enjoy verbal discussions. I have a passion for clarity of understanding, and having to explain my ideas to others allows me the opportunity to refine, organize, and clarify my own thinking. Although I have always viewed verbal communication as a process, until recently I never thought of writing that way. I still recall vividly the time spent writing my dissertation; it was painful and tedious. I used all my creative energy thinking and talking my ideas through and found no purpose in writing. I viewed the writing as "the final word," the product. Each word, therefore, required a great deal of thought before I could get it on paper, and since I had already explained all my ideas to my committee verbally, the final writing seemed fruitless. Eventually I did finish, but with a solemn vow to myself to write very little in the future.

A year later I was asked by a colleague to write a review of Fritjof Capra's book, *The Turning Point*. I acquiesced because I felt the book had tremendous implications for education and the review would be published in a major educational journal. When I had completed the article, I gave it to a colleague at SCSU, for feedback. He returned it to me, saying that he didn't really think it was a book review since it had too many of my own ideas about education in it. I responded with an inquiry about his opinion on my ideas. He explained that, while he thought they were very interesting, they needed expansion for clarification. I invited him to sit and discuss them with me.

"No," he replied. "I know a little about what you think by reading this review. I'll know a little more if we sit and talk. But I'll really understand your ideas when you write about them. If we sit and talk, you won't write. Don't waste your time on book reviews and talking. You have some important ideas to write about. Do it, and the process of writing will make them clearer to you, too."

His comments were painful because I knew the hard work that was ahead of me, but mostly they were painful because I knew he was right. Even though this event occurred several years ago, the incident has remained vivid in my mind because it was the impetus to my beginning development as a writer. He made me feel I had something worthwhile to say, but, even more important, he made me aware that writing was a process.

Like me, most classroom teachers do not view themselves as writers. Because they spend a good deal of their time in a field traditionally based on speech skills, they are usually quite adept and comfortable with oral communication and spend little or no time writing. In order for teachers to empower children as writers, they need to understand the process of writing and know how to encourage and support it, as my colleague did for me. For this reason much of the work I do with teachers in language arts involves empowering them as writers and encouraging them to value the process and to perceive themselves as authors. Excerpts from several classes follow.

"I'd like to get us started tonight by modeling a part of the process that I go through when I write," I began the initial writing session. "First I think about various topics that might have potential and I jot them down." I jotted down "traveling" and explained that I do a great deal of driving in my work and that I might describe the various feelings I have associated with this. Next I explained that a friend from England was visiting me, that I obviously see him infrequently, and that therefore the topic of friendship might be interesting. In a similar fashion, I went on to brainstorm several other topics and wound up with the following list:

> Traveling (work related)
> Friendship (a visiting friend)
> Construction (at present building a house)
> Heat (hot, muggy, July weather in Connecticut)
> Pink (door to the classroom was pink)
> Boxes (what comes in them; different sizes; classrooms are boxes)

From these, I chose the topic of "construction" and began to develop it by making a web (Rico, 1983). I placed the word *construction* in a circle and began free associating. "I'm presently in the midst of building a house," I explained, drawing an arrow out from the circle and writing the words *my house* (see Figure 4.2). "I'm also constantly thinking of all the parts that are being worked on, like the plumbing, the electricity, the framing, and the roofing, and the sequence in which they are structured by the contractor. They're like stages in the process." I then drew an arrow down from the word *house* and wrote *parts: stages* and the four subcategories. I continued associating: "I wonder how the parts will become a whole, but that makes me think of part/whole relations and learning." I kept adding words to the diagram as I spoke. I explained, "When learning, I don't think parts always add up to the whole. Will they with my house? By appearances they seem to, but, no, eventually my house will become a home. That's larger than the sum of the parts, and "home" is an evolving concept. It seems that both building a house *and* learning are roads to adventure. And that reminds me of a sign I saw the other day on a teacher's desk. It read, 'Learning is the road to success.' I'm going to change it. How about, 'The road to knowledge is always under construction'?" I wrote the expression and com-

Figure 4.2.   Web for the topic of "Construction."

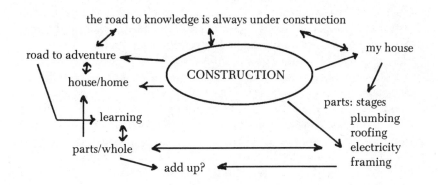

mented, "Yes, I think I'll end my piece with that." The figure shows my finished web.

After students had time to reflect on what they had observed, I explained, "Rather than tell you about it, I modeled this process to show you what I mean by topic generation and webbing. But it is far more important to do it with you now, than it is simply to show you." I then requested that they list some possible topics, choose one, make a web, and find a partner with whom to share it. "What I want you and your partner to do for each other," I continued, "is simply to ask each other questions. Your job as a partner is not to critique or evaluate. Instead, simply try to find out more about what your partner was thinking. The purpose of this activity, called rehearsal, is to help you and your partner think of more and more ideas that will serve as 'grist' for your writing later."

From past experience I have learned that, while the webbing process and subsequent discussion often help generate ideas, many of my students need specific help with generating metaphors. Their webs often are specific and literal. For example, Diane generated several topics, chose to write on "changes," and then brainstormed the web in Figure 4.3. Although Diane touched on some interesting concepts, such as security versus insecurity, and lifetime growth, most of her web described specific physical changes in her life. As I often do, to encourage metaphoric thinking, I engaged students in the following activity.

"I'm going to share some images with you," I began. "See if you can guess the object or concept I'm thinking about." Pausing after each image offered, I listed: silver ribbon, wet runner, laughing path, sun cooler, sweat cleanser, stone mover, land sculptor, woodland tears.

Eventually they guessed that I was thinking of a woodland stream. I then divided the class into small groups of four participants and gave each group a single word, with instructions to develop images for their word, together. The words I used were *trees*, *idea*, *snow*, and *poems*. After working together for about 10 minutes, each group in turn shared their lists while the other groups attempted to guess the word given.

"Let's return to our webs, now," I urged, focusing the class back on their own writing. "I'd like you to think of your topic in the same way, and to help you I'm going to ask you to respond to these four questions: What is it like? How are the two things similar? Of what does it remind me? How do I feel about it?" (These four questions come from a suggested activity in a wonderful little book, *Let Them Write Poetry*, by Walter, 1962.) In response to the questions, Diane wrote,

CHANGES

What is it like?   Time controller/life mover
How are the two things similar?   Both are an intrinsic part of
     life
Of what does it remind me?   Hands pushing and pulling
How do I feel about it?   Feel like putting it all in a box to open
     tomorrow

The traditional view of the teacher's role in writing is simply to

---

Figure 4.3.   Diane's web for the topic of "Changes."

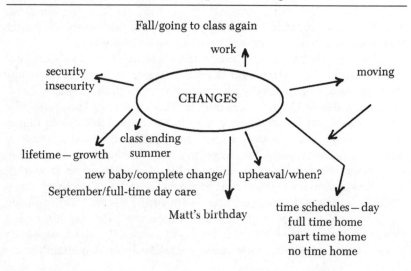

motivate student writing and then respond to it. In contrast, writing process research (Calkins, 1986; Graves, 1983, 1984) shows that teachers also need to facilitate and support drafts and revisions with personal writer's conferences or small-group authors' circles. Toward this aim, I structured a writing period for students to take their webs and begin work on initial drafts. I worked on a piece of writing as well during this time. At the end of the period, I convened an "author's circle" and asked if anyone would like to share his draft. Several read theirs aloud. Diane's was as follows:

> I know in the middle I make the
>   choices
> to stay, to go, to stop, to start.
> But even though I'm there it seems — to
>   take a momentum all its own
> So in the midst I think of all
> I must do that, this for sure. I'll go here and
> Stay right there, the time is now, it won't fit in
> And then I want to put it all away
> and think of it another day

When she concluded, I asked (as I had done after each reader) if there were comments, questions, or suggestions.

"I love the way you described yourself as being in the middle," Hannah responded. "I never would have thought about changes putting me 'in the middle.' But now I can really feel the tugs."

"Yes," Sarah added. "And I can feel it in the rhythm of the poem as well when you pit opposites against each other like, 'to stay, to go, to stop, to start.' I'm curious how you responded to the four questions Cathy asked us."

Diane read her responses to the group, and Sarah picked up on the last one. "Putting it all in a box — I really like that. Why did you decide to make it 'all away' in the poem instead?"

"I really don't know," Diane replied. "Which do you like better?"

"Well, I think the box line is much more unusual," Sarah explained. "Putting it all away for another day is too expected. The box idea gives the reader a new image — it's fresher."

"I never thought about it that way, through the reader's eyes," Diane replied reflectively and with obvious pleasure over the serious manner in which people were taking her poem. The next day she asked if she could read a new draft of her poem.

"I've tried to heighten the rhythm in order to make the image clearer to the reader," she explained, and she shared her latest version:

CHANGES

I know in the middle I make the choices
to stay — to go, to stop — to start
But even though I'm there it seems
to take momentum all its own.
So in the midst I think of all
I must do that — this for sure
I'll go here and stay right there
The time is now — it won't fit in
I'd like to put it in a box
and open it another day.

INVESTIGATING CHILDREN'S WRITING

Parallel to our collection and analysis of children's spelling attempts, I require students to investigate children's writing by each choosing a child to work with throughout the semester. They observe the children, conference with them, and collect samples of their work. By using these data as a focus of class discussion, we have been able to view the full developmental progression of writing from the preschool years to adolescence. Using the research of Calkins (1986) and Graves (1983) as a framework in our investigations and analyses, we have observed the following six stages in the development of creative writing.

Stage 1

Although the young child at this stage has little knowledge of words being made up of letters representing sounds, beginning writing does occur in the form of pictures, oftentimes with letters and numerals added, sprawled across the paper. Rehearsal and writing are inseparable; the child gets ideas by drawing, and the drawing represents the writing. No drafting or editing occur. Figure 4.4 shows Jessica's work at age four, which is characteristic of this stage.

Stage 2

At this stage, rehearsal and writing begin to be differentiated. Drawing serves the purpose of rehearsal, with a phrase or sentence about the picture added. The emphasis during the writing is usually on decoding the sounds and putting them onto paper. As in stage 1, no

Figure 4.4.   Jessica's writing at age 4.

drafting or revision is evident. The work of Dylan at age five years, six months, shown in Figure 4.5, is representative of this stage.

Stage 3

Rehearsal at this stage often shifts back and forth between drawing and talking with a writing partner. The "all about" phrases and sentences also begin to take the form of simple narratives. Stories often begin with "One day" or "Once upon a time;" proceed sequentially in describing what happened first, second, and third (an order that is determined by the event, not the author); and sometimes even end with "The End" scrawled at the bottom of the paper. Beginning attempts at revision may occur, but they are usually only "add-ons" as a result of audience questions or requests for more detail. The following piece, written by Katie at age eight, exemplifies a sequence governed by the event.

THE TWO BEST DAYS EVER

One day I was talking to my friend and I said, "Would you like to hear about baseball?" Melissa said, "Yes." So I started talk-

Figure 4.5.   Dylan's writing at age five years, six months: "I am mow-
ing the grass."

ing. "First the coach gives you a uniform, cap, glove, and we start
the game. Even when it is hot it is fun. Once after a game, right
before I went home, I ran across the field to the stream of water. I
drank a lot." I told Melissa all about baseball until it was time to go
home. The next day I went to school. My teacher said, "We are going to talk about sports. First football, baseball, tennis, golf, swim-
ming, and basketball." After learning about sports we had no time
for reading, spelling, or recess so we got on the bus to go home. I
got off the bus and walked up the driveway and into the house. "Hi
Mom, hi Dad, I'm home," I said. My mom said, "Go to the kitchen
and do your homework." So I did my homework and when I was
done I watched TV until 6:00 o'clock. Then we ate dinner. An
hour later I went to bed.

THE END

Stage 4

The benefit of rehearsal involving webbing or peer discussions is
clearly established at this point, and, although the content and sequence of the piece are still governed by the event being described, the
perspective of the reader or audience begins to be taken into account.

For example, at age nine, Josh began to write by making the web illustrated in Figure 4.6. After an initial draft, some minor revisions in the form of a few inserts, and editing involving checks of spelling and punctuation, he completed the following piece:

> One night I went to a very scary haunted house. It looked frightening. I went inside. It was all red. I smelled it. It was blood! I went upstairs shaking. There were monsters all over the place.
>
> I fell down a hole. It was all dark. I saw that the walls were moving. I saw a door. I went through the door and it shut behind me. It was very loud.
>
> I seemed to remember this place. But what I remembered was a dream. I walked through the hallway. A monster jumped out. It was very frightening. It was green and slimy. I realized none of the monsters were touching me. I found a door. I went out the door and looked around. I saw a sign. It said "Disneyland"!!

Although Josh described in his piece a recent event (he had recently returned from Disneyland) and his narrative was sequential in terms of the physical events he went through, he kept the reader in suspense until the end. He was beginning to use language to communicate feelings to an imagined reader.

Stage 5

A piece representative of stage 5, but too lengthy to be included here was written by Damien (age 13). His main concern in writing the piece centered around topic information. He began with an imaginary trip to another planet, where a secret water was found that maintains youth. The astronaut in the story faced the dilemma of whether or not

Figure 4.6. Josh's web for the topic of "Haunted Houses."

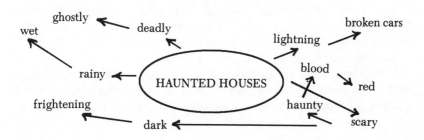

to bring the secret water back to Earth. The setting and event were almost incidental to the dilemma, which formed the focus of the story. Damien's work is typical of stage 5, where stories are controlled by the author, rather than the event. The event, in fact, is chosen to fit the author's intent. At this stage, different leads and endings are tried and revision entails moving, deleting, or adding chunks of text.

Stage 6

Stage 6 is descriptive of the level on which most professional creative writers work. The main focus is on revising and drafting and on establishing a "style." Language is used to develop characters, to provoke emotion in the reader, and to work out inner turmoils and dilemmas.

CONSTRUCTING A PEDAGOGY FOR LANGUAGE ARTS

Although the six stages just discussed are characteristic of qualitatively different ways of thinking about writing, they should not be thought of as discrete or be used to label children or their products. Instead, it is the ability to chart developmental constructions and facilitate the transitions between levels that has the most importance to teachers.

To encourage growth, teachers need to understand the direction of the process. With this objective in mind, I ask them to characterize the shifts they see from stage to stage, in both spelling and writing, and to look for connections between the stages. From experience, I've found that focused reflection on the developmental progression as a whole often brings about some interesting insights in relation to learning.

"The main shift I see," David offered in response to my request, "is the movement toward greater and greater abstractions."

"How so?" Karen asked.

"Well, look at the spelling stages," he began. "Each level requires that the child deal with sounds in a more abstract way. In the beginning it is a direct letter-to-sound match. The shift to patterns requires an inference about the way letter sounds are affected *within* the word. Eventually inferences have to be made in relation to the meaning, and some letter sounds are even negated in the process."

Meg nodded in agreement and added, "And I think perhaps it has to do with making inferences about change; what I mean is, at first the child may know some names or sounds of letters, but they are changed in words. The parts have to be isolated from the whole, and then blended back together as a whole word, and that's hard because blending changes the sounds somewhat. Vowel patterns like *ai* are even more difficult because the *a* completely changes the *i* sound; it leaves it with none. And, finally, like David said, when you get to having to analyze the change by meaning, it's not even the letters or sounds that explain the change but meaning, history, or culture."

"Yes. That's good, Meg. That's the pattern I was trying to describe," David commented with a pleased smile at Meg's understanding.

"Does the same pattern depict the shifts in writing?" I asked, pushing them to make a connection.

After a few minutes of quiet, Amy responded. "Yes, I think it does. I was thinking about the spiral that my group made, to show the history of English, and its connection to the spelling and writing stages. In writing, each new level is a move away from the center, just like the spelling changes in history moved away from pure phonetics. Imagine yourself with raw sounds in the center and at the base of the spiral. You begin by writing about yourself and your experiences; you spell by a direct sound-to-letter match. Then you move away from the center. You begin to be able to take the perspective of the reader into account in writing; in spelling, you realize that patterns govern sound. Finally, language simply becomes a tool, controlled by the author and used to depict abstractions and meaning."

"That's a beautiful metaphor," I commented to Amy, and members of the class nodded in agreement. Challenging them to focus on pedagogy, I probed, "So as teachers, how do we facilitate those shifts? That seems to be the next question."

Pam responded first. "I think the spelling and writing activities that you did with us facilitated that process," she stated emphatically.

"How?" I inquired, encouraging her to reflect on her own experiences as a learner.

"Well, for example, in the spelling activity, I was challenged to think about roots in a way I never had before. I had always thought of roots from my own meaning base; the root of *flexible*, to me, was *flex*. I never thought about early roots; that's a shift away from myself, like Amy described with her spiral representation."

"I felt a similar shift during the metaphor activity," Karen added. "Having to think up metaphors for the word *tree* was challenging, but not only because I had to use my imagination. The hard part was trying to think up images for the listeners that were simultaneously fresh and understandable. If the metaphor was too outlandish, it would only be understood by me; if it was easily understood, it risked being too common. I was constantly trying to put myself in the place of the listener."

"So are you saying these are good activities that you will bring back to your classroom and try?" I asked, allowing them much wait time to think about my question.

"No," Karen finally replied. "They wouldn't be appropriate for my kids." She paused, obviously still reflecting, then continued, "I think they were appropriate for us because they were a slight challenge to the level we were on. I'll speak for myself. Probably, as a writer, I'm around stage four — I usually view writing as a final product and do little revision. I also always thought of writing as 'putting my ideas down on paper.' I don't think I really ever thought about the reader as I was writing. The activities you did were challenges to my way of thinking, because I had to think simultaneously of myself and the reader. They stretched me."

David was nodding in agreement. "Yes," he commented. "It makes me realize the inadequacies of correcting spelling from a stage-5 perspective if the learner is at stage 2. Instead, it seems the role of the teacher needs to involve, first, figuring out how the learner thinks; then, second, providing a challenge to encourage rethinking. You have to be the tug to expand the circle, but the supporter to help the upward shift."

Diane commented, "That reminds me of my poem, David — 'the push and the pull.'"

I nodded and smiled in acknowledgment, then challenged them: "So, shall we put these ideas in a box, or deal with change?"

5

And Greener Still:
Investigations in Mathematics

To understand is to invent.
— Piaget, *To Understand is to Invent*

*The growth of mathematical understanding is perhaps not
to be conceived in terms of a linear progression but as a
loosely determined path through a multi-dimensional lattice
of concepts which are mastered as existing knowledge is
viewed from a new and more enlightened perspective.*
— Rowland, *The Enquiring Classroom*

The discipline to which the greatest disservice occurs in the schools is
perhaps mathematics. Unfortunately, it is often taught solely as arithmetical computation, with little or no attempt made at facilitating
reasoning or the development of logic. Children spend hours practicing
algorithms that they often don't understand. The deeper concepts such
as place value, part-to-whole relations, and the distributive property
are often assumed to be understood, as long as the child is computing
successfully.

Teachers may be at fault for teaching mathematics from this perspective, but oftentimes they know no better since they themselves are
products of a similar approach. As learners, they frequently sat in math
classes and practiced procedures, proofs, and calculations. They learned
to memorize and regurgitate these procedures and rarely were given
concrete materials to make the abstract notation meaningful. The result
is that many teachers do not understand the concepts they are expected
to teach and thus rely on workbook pages, computation sheets, and drill
as common instructional practices for the safety they provide.

Based on the principles outlined in Chapter 2, the Summermath
for Teachers program first provides new mathematical experiences for

inservice teachers, on their level, in order to confront them with "mathematical concepts and problems that they have not encountered before, increase their mathematical knowledge, and have them experience the depth of learning that the constructivist learning environment can encourage" (Simon & Schifter, 1988, p. 5). Discussion and reflection on pedagogy ensue from these experiences, encouraging teachers to question their fundamental assumptions about mathematical learning as well as their habitual patterns of teaching. The dialogue that follows, documenting this program, was taken from the 1986 and 1987 institutes.

TEACHERS AS LEARNERS: CONSTRUCTING
MATHEMATICAL CONCEPTS

Number Systems

"There is a culture," Summermath director Marty Simon began, "which I invite you to pretend to be a part of with me, where the symbols a, b, c, d, and so on, through z, are used for counting." Holding up his fingers to demonstrate numerosity, he continued, "A stands for one thing, b for two, and so on. Any amount more than z is just termed 'many.' There was a young, brilliant mathematician in the society who had invented a way to count, using only 0, a, b, c, and d. Unfortunately, she became ill and died before she could explain her system, but I have with me authentic replicas of the materials found in her hut." At this point, Marty passed out base-5 blocks, shown in Figure 5.1. He continued, "I invite you to form research groups of three or four people to work on inventing a number system, using these materials, which will allow the society to count — even up to 'many' — by only using 0, a, b, c, and d. There will be a mathematical conference held tomorrow in order for the research groups to explain their inventions."

As the participants formed small working groups and began to investigate the problem, Marty and the other staff members moved around listening to the reasoning and asking probing questions. To insure that participants would experience the full impact of the activity, with its parallel nature to children learning place value, participants and staff members were only allowed to use the language of 0, a, b, c, and so on, through z. No explanations that were mere translations of our base-10 system were accepted.

One group began the task by matching each of the letters in the alphabet with a quantity represented by the base-5 materials, and pro-

Figure 5.1. Base-5 blocks.

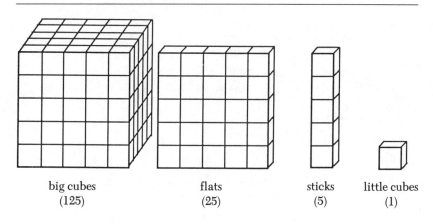

big cubes	flats	sticks	little cubes
(125)	(25)	(5)	(1)

duced the chart illustrated in Figure 5.2. Noticing the patterns that occurred, the group decided to rename the stick *A0*, thus *e* became equal to *A0*, with *f* equal to *A0a*, and *g* equal to *A0b*, and so forth. The flat was named *B00*, and the big cube, *C000*. Although they used *0* in their labels, they did not seem to be using it in a place-value scheme; it was simply part of the label.

Kate, a first-grade teacher and one of the members of the group, was quite excited by the system and suggested they now use it to write each number. They recorded the following: *a, b, c, d, A0, A0a, A0b, A0c, A0d, A0A0, A0A0a, A0A0b, A0A0c, A0A0d, A0A0A0, A0A0A0a, A0A0A0b, A0A0A0c, A0A0A0d, A0A0A0A0*, and so on.

As their numbers grew to larger quantities, the notation also became more extensive, and eventually one of the members, Jeff, commented, "This system might work but I don't think it's more efficient than *a* through *z*. Imagine what the quantity 299 will look like in our notation — *C000C000B00A0A0A0A0d* — and it gets worse with even larger quantities!" Dismayed, his research group partners agreed.

After some thought, a third member, Carol, suggested they put *a, b, c,* or *d* before *B00* to show the number of *A0s* that were missing, for example, 23 would be equal to *aB00c*, instead of *A0A0A0A0c*, because it was one stick short of a flat.

"Like in Roman numerals," commented Kate. At that, the group suddenly realized that their whole invented system was very similiar to the Roman system. They began to investigate the Roman system further,

Figure 5.2. Concrete equivalences using single letters and base-5 blocks, for numbers up to 26.

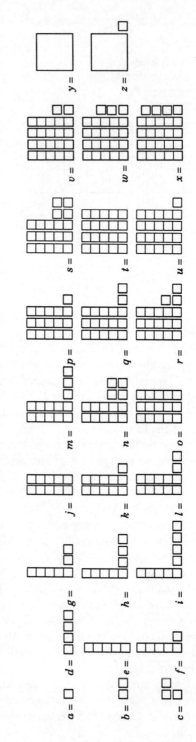

74

comparing similarities to and differences with their system, and then shared their discoveries with Ellen, a staff member, when she joined the group.

After listening with enthusiasm to the group's invention, Ellen suggested they use their system to do some operations, such as addition, multiplication, or division. They agreed and set off with excitement.

A second group, composed of Susan, James, Patty, and Darlene, had begun the task by initially using the blocks to count. When they reached the point of using the sticks for groups of fives, they had also decided to rename the sticks. James, a fifth-grade teacher from Colorado, suggested they call the units A, the sticks B, and the flat and big cubes, C and D, respectively.

Patty, a first-grade teacher from Connecticut, disagreed. "No, that doesn't make sense," she explained. "The stick has a worth of E (5), not B (2). I think we should call it E, but then what will we do for the flat and the big cube?"

After much discussion, Darlene voiced the opinion that the letters A, B, C, and D should represent 1, 2, 3, and 4, respectively; however, their use should not be confined to representing units but should extend to other "columns" in the base-5 system as well. Thus, rather than use B (James's idea) or E (Patty's idea) to represent 5, Darlene proposed that they use $A0$, where the A would mean "1 five" to "1 stick," and the 0 would mean "0 ones." As she noted, all the letters could implicitly stand for units within columns, and "members of the culture would just have to learn the values of the columns." With joviality, consensus was reached, and the group then recorded the chart shown in Figure 5.3.

Confident of the inherent efficiency and consistency of their system, the group decided to try using it with multiplication. Arbitrarily, they chose to multiply $AA \times AA$ and arranged the blocks to represent the problem, then traded to get an answer of ABA, as shown in Figure 5.4. Curious what patterns they would find, they consecutively arranged $AA \times BB$ and then traded to get a result of BDB, as shown in Figure 5.5.

James became very excited: "Look, there is a pattern happening! The middle number is double the end numbers . . . hmmm . . . but that's only going to work until we have to trade up more. $AA \times CC$ will require a further trade, but the pattern does hold if you don't trade completely." He laid out $AA \times CC$ to demonstrate that the number of sticks was double the number of flats and cubes, which were equal (see Figure 5.6).

Susan, a second-grade teacher from Ohio, commented that she saw a different pattern occurring. She separated one of the CC groups (see Figure 5.7) and explained that it was a representation of $A \times CC$. She

(text continued on page 78)

Figure 5.3. Concrete equivalences using letter combinations to construct a place-value system for base-5 blocks.

0	A	B	C	D
A0	AA	AB	AC	AD
B0	BA	BB	BC	BD
C0	CA	CB	CC	CD
D0	DA	DB	DC	DD
A00	A0A	A0B	A0C	A0D
AA0	AAA	AAB	AAC	AAD
AB0	ABA	ABB	ABC	ABD
AC0	ACA	ACB	ACC	ACD
AD0	ADA	ADB	ADC	ADD
B00	B0A	B0B	B0C	B0D

Figure 5.4. $AA \times AA = ABA$.

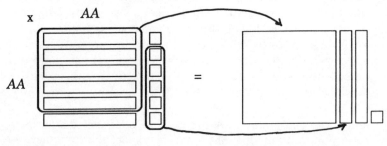

original representation   after the trade

Figure 5.5. $AA \times BB = BDB$.

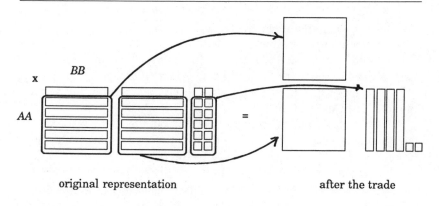

original representation   after the trade

Figure 5.6. $AA \times CC$, with incomplete trade producing 3 flats, 6 sticks, and 3 cubes.

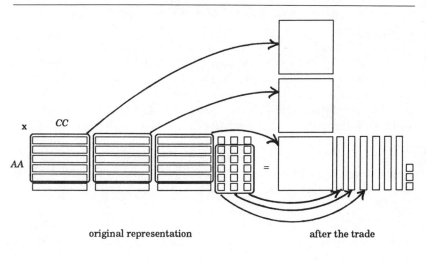

original representation   after the trade

Figure 5.7. Illustrating the distributive property.

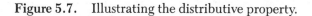

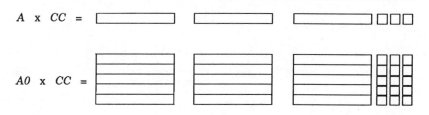

then pushed the remaining pieces together, and, measuring them with a stick, she demonstrated that the remainder was $A0 \times CC$. "What we're really doing," she declared, "is multiplying two parts of the problem and then adding them together. In this case we are adding $(A \times CC) + (A0 \times CC)$, which equals $CC + CC0$. It's the distributive property in action!" she concluded with a flourish.

"Oh, right!" exclaimed Patty. "You know, this is embarrassing to admit, but for years I've taught children that when you multiply 10 times anything, you just add a zero to the number as a place holder. Until this moment, I don't think I fully understood why."

Marty, having just joined the group, heard Patty's admission and asked her to explain what she now understood. "Well," she began, "when you multiply an amount by any amount of sticks, the units will always be an even amount for trading into sticks. In this case the sticks are worth 5 units, and since 5×3 is the same as 3×5, the units are equal to 3 sticks. Because of the commutative property, it will always be an even trade with no units left over." She demonstrated with the examples shown in Figure 5.8.

Marty asked for a paraphrase of Patty's explanation, to make sure that all members of her group had understood. He then commented that a search for patterns was an interesting approach to investigating multiplication and suggested they continue with their inquiry. Pleased with their progress so far, the group decided to use Susan's method of sorting problems into parts and tried $AB \times ACB$, illustrated in Figure 5.9.

"This is great," exclaimed James, "but it would help me to go back to simple multiplication tables and look for patterns so that I don't have to count each time." Members of the group agreed, and they decided to

Figure 5.8.   Illustrating the commutative property.

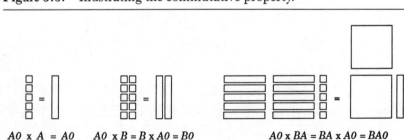

$A0 \times A = A0$ $A0 \times B = B \times A0 = B0$ $A0 \times BA = BA \times A0 = BA0$

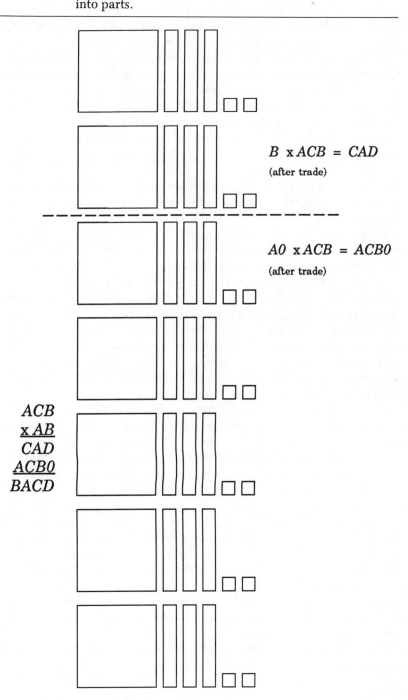

$B \times ACB = CAD$

(after trade)

$A0 \times ACB = ACB0$

(after trade)

ACB
x AB
CAD
ACB0
BACD

record the tables on their original counting sheet. They began with the *D* table, circling each product as shown in Figure 5.10.

"Wonderful!" James grinned when they had finished. "I won't have to memorize the *D* table. Look at the pattern. As the digit on the right decreases by one, the digit on the left increases by one." He paused and then mused with obvious curiosity, "Why is that? . . . Oh, I see . . . The table is based on fives. We are adding fours, so we lose one each time we add another row." He answered his own question with obvious self-satisfaction.

The group was excited by their discovery and went on to explore the *B* and *C* tables. They recorded the products of the *B* table with circles and placed boxes around the products of the *C* table, as shown in Figure 5.11.

"The fact that the patterns are all diagonals surprises me," Patty ventured. "I've done this before with base 10 and gotten straight lines for the twos table." She paused, obviously perplexed.

"That's because none of our numbers go evenly into five, which is our base," explained Susan. "Ten divides evenly by two and five; there is no remainder. It's the remainder that produces the diagonal." Susan looked at Patty, who was nodding now in agreement. Then she went on, "What interests me is the pattern of common multiples; it increases by a stick and a cube each time: *AA, BB, CC, DD*—" Susan paused, trying to make sense of the pattern *AA0, ABA, ACB, ADC, B0D* and its connection to the *AA, BB, . . . DD* pattern.

"Let's check and see what *EE* would be," offered James, laying out *E* sticks and *E* cubes. They traded up and discovered that *EE* was equal to *AA0*.

"Oh, I get it," Patty began with excitement. "The pattern is *AA, BB, CC, . . . ZZ*. Each time you add a stick and a cube, because that amount is worth six (five plus one) and six is the least common multiple of two and three."

James was now visibly excited, too. "Oh, that's great, Patty," he declared. "What a shortcut! To find a series of common multiples for any given numbers, you find the least common multiple of the numbers and that times table produces your series. For example, the series of common multiples of 2 and 4 is the 4 times table; for 3 and 5, it's the 15 table; for 6 and 2, it's the 6 table." After pausing, with a smile he added, "I feel like a reborn mathematician. I always thought of math as computation. It was tedious and boring. This is exciting!"

Other members of the group acknowledged his comment with agreement.

Figure 5.10. The D multiplication table.

0	A	B	C	D
A0	AA	AB	AC	AD
B0	BA	BB	BC	BD
C0	CA	CB	CC	CD
D0	DA	DB	DC	DD
A00	A0A	A0B	A0C	A0D
AA0	AAA	AAB	AAC	AAD
AB0	ABA	ABB	ABC	ABD
AC0	ACA	ACB	ACC	ACD
AD0	ADA	ADB	ADC	ADD
B00	B0A	B0B	B0C	B0D

Figure 5.11. The *B* and *C* multiplication tables.

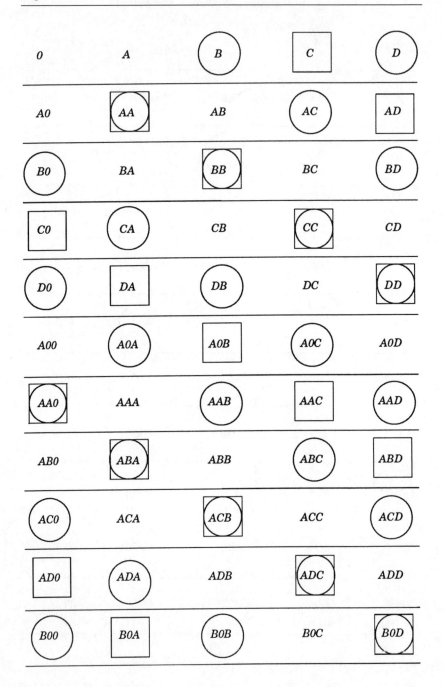

Periodicity

While the activity that occurs in small research groups is important, much is also gained in the process of sharing ideas afterward. Eleanor Duckworth (1987a) speaks to this issue:

> Instead of explaining to the students, I ask them to explain what they think and why. I find the following results. First, in trying to make their thoughts clear for other people, students achieve greater clarity for themselves. Much of the learning is in the explaining. (Why should the teacher monopolize occasions for trying to make herself clear?) Second, the students themselves determine what it is they want to understand. It is not only the explanations that come from them, but also the questions. Third, people come to depend on themselves: They are the judges of what they know and believe. They know why they believe it, what questions they still have about it, their degree of uncertainty about it, what they want to know next about it, how it relates to what other people think. Any other "explanation" they encounter must establish its place within what they know. Fourth, students recognize the powerful experience of having their ideas taken seriously, rather than simply screened for correspondence to what the teacher wanted. Fifth, students learn an enormous amount from each other. Finally, learners come to recognize knowledge as a human construction, since they have constructed their own knowledge and they know that they have. [pp. 130–131]

With these aims in mind, Marty convened the "math congress" for a sharing and discussion of ideas. Most of the research groups had invented number systems similar either to a Roman numeral system or incorporating place value. The systems were shared, critiqued, discussed, and used to perform operations such as addition and multiplication, with most participants concluding that the place-value system was more efficient and easier to use.

Eileen, a fifth-grade teacher from New Hampshire, was visibly excited and asked if she could explain a discovery she had had during the activity. She went to the chalkboard and drew the picture reproduced in Figure 5.12. Explaining her drawing, she began, "After we constructed a place-value system, I began playing around with decimals and multiplication. I called the big cube my unity, or my unit, and realized that the decimals would become flats, then sticks, and then little cubes, ad infinitum. When I put in my commas and thought about what the shapes of those numbers would be, I suddenly realized that the shapes

Figure 5.12. Illustrating periodicity.

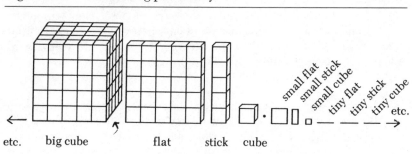

formed a repeating pattern around the commas." She added the shapes to her drawing and then went on. "My concept of how numbers grow had always been linear, not geometric; I had always been adding one. It had never occurred to me that our whole number system, no matter which base is used, forms repeating *geometric* patterns, even with decimals."

"Why does that happen?" Marty probed.

"It's the squaring—" Eileen paused, not sure of her answer.

Josh, a seventh-grade math teacher who had been deep in reflection, extended Eileen's discovery by offering, "And then cubing, then multiplying by the base, then squaring, then cubing, and so on. With decimals it's the same process, but with fractions." He came to the board and drew the following, explaining that N stood for the base being used:

$$N^6 \ N^5 \ N^4 \ N^3 \ N^2 \ N^1 \ 1 \quad \bullet \quad 1/_{N^1} \ 1/_{N^2} \ 1/_{N^3} \ 1/_{N^4} \ 1/_{N^5} \ 1/_{N^6}$$

James was puzzled. "I see what you're saying, Josh, but if we were to continue putting the commas in through the decimals, starting from the unit and counting 3 columns, the first comma would be after the second decimal digit, not the third."

"That's true, James," Eileen commented. "My students ask me a similar question, and I've never known how to answer them. They always ask me why there are no 'oneths,' and just now, I think I've realized what the problem is. We've always thought of the decimal point as the pivot. It isn't, though; the unit is." Eileen paused, and then with a smile she continued, "It's kind of 'Zen'; if I'm the unit, anything to the left of me is positive or whole, and anything to the right of me is negative, or fractional."

"Oh, that's great, Eileen," Josh said excitedly. "And the superscript tells how many zeroes there are." He paused and then wrote the following:

$$10^2 = 100 \qquad 10^{-1} = 1/10 = .1$$
$$10^3 = 1000 \qquad 10^{-2} = 1/100 = .01$$
$$10^4 = 10,000 \qquad 10^{-3} = 1/1000 = .001$$

"I've seen scientists write numbers that way," he concluded, "but I never knew why."

The enthusiasm in the class was clearly at a peak. "I can't wait to explain what I've learned about decimals to my fifth graders in the fall," exclaimed Eileen. "Maybe it will help them understand decimals better, too."

"And would that be any better than what teachers presently do now?" I probed. "Don't we presently 'tell' and 'show' beautiful systems and understandings that brilliant mathematicians before us have constructed?"

The class was quiet. Then Susan thoughtfully responded, "You're right, Cathy. It would be no different. Not that we shouldn't share it, but the power in this lesson came from the fact that we constructed these ideas ourselves. This is probably some of the highest-level math thinking I've done in years. In college I had courses in calculus and algebra, but they were all abstract, and I simply memorized procedures to solve problems; I didn't really understand what I was doing. Today, I feel empowered, challenged, and excited about mathematics." She paused, then added, "My question, though, is how do we achieve this with our students?" The next section presents our examination of this question.

INVESTIGATIONS AND REFLECTIONS ON LEARNING

Teachers As Epistemologists

An important process for teachers after their investigations in a content area is reflection on their own learning. By analyzing the process they have just gone through, teachers begin to construct an understanding of how knowledge develops. This forming epistemology serves as the "grist" in the development of pedagogy.

Toward this aim, Marty responded to Susan's question by turning the responsibility for answering it back to the participants. "Research," he began, "shows that kids think mathematics consists of a bunch of unrelated facts, procedures, and computations. Perhaps the first general aim is to enable connections; instead of teaching isolated bits of knowledge, we need to facilitate a network of relationships. The mathematical foundation needs to be strong and solid, and for that to have occurred kids need to have expanded on what they know by taking time to investigate and make inferences. If we simply 'give' the foundation, it is apt to be linear and shaky. Kids end up in special-needs classes, often because we keep giving them walls and roofs on a shaky foundation." He paused to give people time to think about what he had said and then went on. "Susan has asked an important question. Let's deal with it by reflecting on our own learning. What did the staff do to enable you to feel empowered?"

Megan, a fifth-grade teacher from Massachusetts, raised her hand and addressed her words to the staff. "I'm sure that you probably did plan for us to solve the problem with a place-value system, but it didn't feel that way. It really felt like shared discovery, that there was no answer in particular that you were looking for. In fact, I want to change the word 'discover' to 'invent,' because discovery is the uncovering of what someone else wants you to find. Invention is more powerful and connotes ownership. I felt like I owned the solution."

Murmurs of agreement were heard around the room, and Marty asked, "If there were two children, one of whom had figured out for herself how to do a certain type of problem, whereas the other had been shown, whom would you bet on to solve successfully a slightly different but similar problem?" Unanimously, the class agreed that they would bet on the child who had figured it out herself. Marty went on, "Isn't it interesting that, as teachers, we all bet that way, yet schools still teach as if they believed the other?"

"That's because it requires a lot of risk taking on the teacher's part," responded Kate. "And you really have to trust the learner."

Marty asked her to explain. She continued, "As a teacher, you don't always know where the lesson is going to go; it depends on the learner's needs. You can't have your lessons all planned, and that's scary."

James was intently pondering the conversation. Slowly, still in thought, he began, "I've been thinking that one of the things we do as teachers, that I realize now is erroneous, is that we make assumptions that kids know certain things when we see them use the algorithms successfully, and we also think that because *we* 'covered' a certain concept, they should know it."

"It's a bit like a collusion, isn't it?" Marty responded. "We implicitly say, 'we'll teach you to act like you know it, and you act that way,' and then both parties carry on their agreements. I used to teach seventh and eighth graders, and invariably I would get students doing the following with the problem, $3^1/_4$ minus $1^3/_4$. Because they couldn't take $^3/_4$ from $^1/_4$, they would borrow a 1 from the 3 and put the 1 in front of the $^1/_4$, making $^{11}/_4$. Subtracting $^3/_4$ from $^{11}/_4$ produced $^8/_4$, or 2. Adding the 2 to the 1, they would get an answer of 3. As 'good' students would do, they had remembered what they had learned and carried it over to what they were now being taught! Now, we should give those students credit, because they have carried over and extended what they already knew!" Laughter was heard around the class. Marty went on, "We *should* have a serious talk with their teachers, because clearly in six years of elementary school these students had not understood regrouping, the basis of place value. And, as a little aside, it didn't even bother them that they were taking nearly 2 away from a little over 3 and getting 3! But that's an even different problem." The laughter had subsided with the impact of the truth in Marty's words.

After a period of quiet, Susan mused aloud, "One thing I've learned today is that we can't make the assumption that learners always have the background to learn the concepts we're required to teach."

Marty picked up on her comment. "And so what do you do?" he asked.

"I don't know," she responded. "I guess, review."

"May I push you a little?" Marty asked. She consented, and he continued. "How do you know your review has helped?"

"Test . . . maybe?" She was not satisfied with her answer.

Mary Ellen, also a teacher from Susan's school district, disagreed. "No," she said shaking her head. "That's been the problem all along. Kids can mimic back what you've told them as well as learn procedures that you've shown them to perform computations successfully. But success is not analogous to understanding, and tests usually only assess success with algorithms. We need to probe, asking them to explain verbally what they are doing when they solve problems, maybe even have them teach us. If they can teach the concept, then you know they understand it."

James, in agreement, added, "But only if they can teach and explain using manipulatives to prove their solutions or reasoning. If they can't solve a problem with manipulatives, then you know they are just manipulating numbers and don't understand what they are doing." Quiet ensued, with participants reflecting on the comments of Mary Ellen and James.

"I have a question," Marcy, a third-grade teacher from New York, broke the silence. "I've been thinking about the type of probing questions the staff asked as they came around, and it seems to me that the questions were designed to get us to probe our own understanding, rather than to lead us to an answer."

"That's true, Marcy," Marty responded. "I really do not assume that I know how my students are doing a problem, and I genuinely probe to find out. I'm also not interested in leading my students to a 'right' answer, because I'm probing for understanding, and if I've led you to an answer with a question, I don't know whether you really understand the concept or not. Second, there's some interesting research related to your observation, Marcy, which I'd like to share. Jack Lochhead (1977), at the University of Massachusetts, began a study of strategies used in problem solving. He simply gave college students some math problems to solve, and, as they were working, he asked them to explain their thinking aloud. He also asked questions about their thinking in order to understand more fully what they were doing. To his surprise, the subjects in his study thanked him after the session, remarking that they had learned a great deal of mathematics from him. He was astounded, since he had not attempted to teach anything! From that early work, he went on to study the effect of probing questions on learners and found evidence that simply asking learners to explain their thinking enabled them to advance to higher levels of understanding. It seems that asking questions about thinking causes people to think more. In contrast, leading questions by teachers usually result in a guessing game, with learners trying to figure out what the teacher wants. The learner's thinking moves away from the problem and focuses on the teacher."

"It seems like you're saying that peers are as important as the teacher," James commented on Marty's explanation. "I know that I felt that when I was working with my research group. At one point I was feeling very frustrated because we had moved to the abstract and I wasn't ready; I still needed more concrete experience with the blocks. My group was wonderfully supportive. It made me realize how important group dynamics are. How do we get kids to do that for each other?"

At first there was quiet, then Eva, a kindergarten teacher from Connecticut, broke the silence. "Just *let* them," she blurted out. "On the kindergarten level I see children who love to help each other. I think it's the schools that reinforce competitiveness with our emphasis on the individual, on testing, and on grades. I've never understood why. There is so much power in learning together."

Probing Children's Understanding

While it is important for teachers to engage in investigation and invention with mathematics and then reflect on their own learning, in order really to make connections between themselves, as learners, and the children with whom they work, they also need experience investigating children's understanding. Such investigation serves two purposes. First, when teachers discover the misconceptions children have of the material they have "covered," their scheme of "I covered it, they should know it" is contradicted. This discovery is often stressful, but growth does not occur until teachers let go of the notion that teaching is telling, albeit telling well.

Second, during the process of investigating children's understanding, teachers also develop the ability to question better. In general, teachers are usually quite skilled and practiced in asking questions, but these are mainly of the leading type, pushing children to seek the one "right" answer the teacher desires. It is quite another task to ask non-leading questions of learners, in an attempt to uncover misunderstanding. Toward that aim, the Summermath program requires that teachers work with children on a one-to-one basis, using manipulatives to probe their reasoning and level of understanding of certain math concepts, after which the teachers design lessons that encourage the "invention" of those concepts.

Many interesting interviews were collected, but to relate them all in this chapter is impossible. I will describe in detail one interview by Susan, with a second grader named Peter, in order to illustrate the kind of powerful learning and investigating that went on.

Susan began by asking Peter what he had been studying lately in math. He explained that he had learned to add big numbers like $38+47$ and that he knew how to carry. Susan asked him if he would show her how to do the problem using the blocks. He began counting the unit cubes to get 38 but ran out of materials (he miscounted, anyway). Susan asked him if he could use the sticks to make the numbers. He thought for a minute and then said that he could and put out three sticks and eight cubes, then four sticks and seven cubes. He seemed proud of himself and explained that the sticks were worth 10 each. He then counted up the total of blocks by adding the sticks together first, saying "70," then added the ones to that by counting, "71, 72, . . . 85."

"You said something before about carrying," Susan noted, "Where did you do that?"

"Oh, no," Peter explained. "That's different. That's when you do it on paper—like this." He wrote 38+47, and wrote a 5 in the units column and a 1 in the tens column. He explained that 15 was too big to go in the units column, so you had to put the 1 in the tens column and the 5 in the units column.

"Oh, I see," Susan feigned ignorance. "Do you think we could try to do that with the blocks?"

"Maybe," Peter replied. "I'll try." He rearranged the blocks to show 38+47 again and explained that the 8 and 7 made 15. To represent the 15, he put 5 more units under the 7 and 1 unit above the 3. Susan asked him what the cube above the 3 was for, and he explained that it was the 1 he had carried. He then totaled the amount, disregarding the 8+7 since he had represented that total with 6 cubes. He added the tens first and then the ones, and arrived at 76. He looked puzzled. "Something's wrong," he commented quizzically. "Hmm . . . I don't know. I guess you can't do it this way with the blocks."

Astounded that Peter saw no connection between the concrete representation and the abstract notation, Susan decided to explore his concrete understanding of simple addition and subtraction and asked him to show her 3+6 with the blocks. He did this easily, grouping 3 first, then 6. Pushing them together, he exclaimed, "9." Susan asked if it mattered whether they added 6+3, or 3+6. Peter was sure that it didn't. Susan asked him to prove that to her, using the blocks. Peter thought for quite a while, then came up with quite a nice proof. He laid out the 3 and the 6, side by side, as illustrated in Figure 5.13. Drawing a circle around 3 and then 6, he read it left to right and declared that the whole was 9. Keeping the cubes there, he did the same right to left, showing that the whole didn't change.

Susan exclaimed that he had indeed convinced her and mused, "I wonder if it works for subtraction?"

"Oh yes," Peter assured her, and he grabbed the paper and pencil again, writing 7−5=2 and 5−7=2. "See," he said, proudly waving the paper in front of her.

Susan asked him to show her with the blocks. He put out 7 and then removed 5. "There!" he said definitively.

"What about the second part, 5−7?" Susan asked.

"You can't do that one with the blocks," Peter declared, "but it is the same. See—" and he pointed to the paper again.

"Why can't we do it with the blocks?" Susan probed.

Peter was undaunted. "Because you can't take 7 away if you've only got 5," he declared, still totally oblivious to the connection between the concrete (the blocks) and the abstract (the numbers)!

The interview goes on with Susan continuing to probe. She later

Figure 5.13.   Peter's proof.

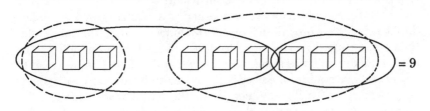

designed some lessons around the concepts of subtraction and place value, using the manipulatives with meaningful word problems. The description of various lessons during classroom teaching is for another chapter; the importance of this synopsis is that it suffices to illustrate how the uncovering of children's misconceptions in mathematics serves as a powerful force in motivating participants to look critically at their prior schemes about teaching.

After the interview, Susan, shaking her head in amazement, commented to me, "I realize now that manipulatives are valuable and necessary at all levels of instruction. I'd heard before in lecture and discussion classes for teachers, 'use manipulatives'; but it wasn't until this program, when I needed to use them as a learner, and today when I saw Peter having that same need, that I really understood their necessity."

Susan was relating her experience as a learner to Peter's and she was beginning the important construction of a pedagogy appropriate to the needs of the learner, to understanding, and to empowerment.

SUMMARY

This chapter has described an inservice mathematics program for teachers. Although the math content here dealt with place value, it should not be difficult to imagine higher-level liberal-arts math courses, team taught with math educators in a similar fashion. If mathematics, where possible, were taught from the concrete to the abstract in such a way as to empower learners, those learners, as eventual classroom teachers themselves, would have powerful experiences with which to construct their own pedagogy.

Much more could be said about the learning that occurs when teachers have the world of mathematics opened to them and attempt to facilitate that experience with their students, but perhaps this declaration from one of the participants is sufficient:

"My biggest difficulty as a learner was realizing that language didn't help; the words didn't mean anything . . . only the manipulatives made sense. I needed them to think. In the future I'm going to be at the chalkboard far less often because when I'm there I know I tend to be verbal. I've realized the need for children to be involved with physical investigation, to be challenged. In the past I made kids feel the manipulatives were a crutch; they were only for those who needed help. I want instead, now, to challenge my students with them. I feel like a reborn mathematician, and I want my students to feel that way, too."

6

Taking Root:
A Case Study

The likelihood that professional study will affect what powerful early experiences have inscribed on the mind and emotions will depend on its power to cultivate images of the possible and desirable and to forge commitments to make those images a reality.

— Nemser, "Learning to Teach"

Can a teacher acquire a constructivist perspective after many years of being a learner in classes taught from a traditional, transmission perspective? And if so, what process facilitates and supports such change? Whereas the last three chapters described examples of possible course work in the preservice component of a teacher-education program, this chapter focuses on the foregoing questions by documenting the process of change that one teacher, Jill Lester, went through during the year following such course work. As such, it also provides an illustration of the mentoring process that might take place during an internship year, as suggested in Chapter 2.

JILL

Background

Jill, a 38-year-old mother of two, had recently returned to full-time classroom teaching after a long tenure as homemaker and substitute teacher, when she applied to the Summermath for Teachers program at Mount Holyoke College. She was accepted and consequently enrolled in the 1986 institute (described in Chapter 5).

On her application she stated that she had graduated in 1969 from a small state college in Rhode Island with a B.S. in elementary education. Her program there had been conventional in that, after taking various liberal-arts courses taught mostly in lecture fashion, she had enrolled in the college's education program and subsequently completed traditional methods courses and student teaching. Upon graduating and getting married, she had taught for two and a half years but then had resigned with plans to start a family. After seven years of full-time homemaking and another five years substituting in various public schools, she had applied for and gotten a full-time position in a private, alternative, progressive elementary school. Although she had begun the year with great excitement, the demands for alternative methods had been high. While she had recognized the value in them, she had felt confused and anxious from the lack of specific direction given her to implement such a program. At the end of the year, when her contract expired, she had returned to full-time substituting. A year later, she had assumed a more conventional, first-grade, public school position with a class size of 20 in a rural Berkshire setting. After a year of "successful" teaching there, she had applied to the Summermath for Teachers program with the expressed purpose "to learn and share ideas with other professionals, explore new concepts, develop more confidence in trying new techniques, and to have information and enthusiasm to bring back and share with my colleagues."

Philosophy of Teaching at the Start

At the beginning of the program, Jill's teaching style was fairly conventional. For reading instruction she had used basals and workbooks and had children grouped by levels. For mathematics instruction she relied on a standard text and had children proceed through workbooks and activities, interspersed with some manipulative experiences. The curriculum sequence in all subjects was determined by the texts, with the exception of journal writing, which she had begun with a great deal of success. She had also taught herself LOGO and then taken a graduate class in its use in the classroom. Although she had not yet used it, her commitment to including it in her math program was high.

Jill's *practice* was conventional, but she seemed to have an intuitive, albeit unformed, vision of what teaching could be. She simply had no idea how to get there. Evidence for this appeared in Jill's response on her application to a request to describe a favorite classroom lesson:

One of my favorite math lessons was actually a happy accident. My goal was to introduce the concept of "tens and ones" to my first-grade children. I began the lesson with envelopes of plastic markers for each child. Each envelope contained markers numbering any- where from 11 to 19. Each child was directed to open his/her enve- lope and to count out 10 markers, group them, and determine how many were 'left over.' We wrote the numerals on the board, and dis- cussed how many tens and how many ones there are in 17 or 14 or 12, and so forth. After about 10 minutes of exploration, a child shouted out, 'I'll bet that will work for bigger numbers, too!' We tried it with larger groups of markers, and the children were excit- ed about their 'new discovery.' In one lesson, most of my 20 chil- dren grasped the concept of 'tens and ones' and were able to apply the concept to numbers ranging from 11 to 99.

Jill clearly seemed to be aware of the value of discovery and had described a lesson encouraging reflection and inquiry, yet to her it was a "happy accident." Although she could intuitively recognize good teach- ing when it happened, how to structure experiences to facilitate such events on a daily basis was still a mystery.

Participation in Summermath for Teachers Institute

Jill was an involved and highly motivated participant during the two-week math institute and by the end of the first week had made some astute observations of her own learning process. In her first synthesis paper, she wrote,

This week has been an experience that will live with me for a long time. It has been challenging. It has been exhilarating. It has been exhausting.
Through the week's program, I have learned a great deal about myself and my own style of learning. I have found myself learning from my own errors. With the understanding of the errors in my thinking, I have gained greater understandings of the con- cepts involved. Thus came the discovery that the correct answer isn't nearly as important as the thought process.

Jill also reflected on the value of peer interaction:

My newest awareness of myself is the need that I have of some pri- vate space when I am learning. I find that I am resentful when I have to share my experiences with others before I have come to terms with them on my own. . . . Yet, I've also learned that ex- plaining of one's thought process requires a great deal of under- standing. I've learned much from listening to my colleagues and by having to explain my thought processes to them.

And perhaps most important, Jill had made note of the self-regulatory nature of learning:

> I have noticed that the specific needs of the learner determine what the individual learner might discover from a task. For example, the pattern block activity was designed for the whole group, yet each of us interpreted the activity to fit into our individual fields of knowledge. . . . Learning LOGO is another example of this. Each day, I approach class with a personal goal. I find that, as I attempt to program, new needs arise. Although I am working in a group setting, I have my own agenda . . . so do children.

By the end of the first week, Jill had made some important connections between learning and pedagogy that enabled her vision of good teaching to become clearer. Yet, as the second week progressed and she began to think about how to facilitate such mathematical learning in her second-grade classroom, her clarity and assuredness became a bit more tenuous. In her second synthesis paper, she described how she felt somewhat overwhelmed and thus chose to focus on only two strategies during the upcoming year.

> This week has taken on a different focus for me. How much of what I have learned can realistically be assimilated into my teaching style? . . . The two days that we spent with individual children afforded me a completely safe environment for trying out my new learnings. For example, as the time for teaching approached, I listened to many new ideas. (Why I had not thought of some of them remains a mystery.) I latched onto the idea of beginning with meaningful word problems as a stepping-stone for the work with manipulatives. As I reflect back on last year's teaching, I can visualize my classroom bustling with activity as the children used manipulatives. Yet, I smile when I realize that as soon as I felt that *I* knew the concept, the manipulatives disappeared. (Didn't I know the concept before I began? How fair was I being to the children?) I feel, now, that I know how I will try to apply my new learnings to the classroom. Two modifications are about all I can handle at one time. The addition of manipulatives (that don't disappear into boxes on the shelves) will be the easier of the two changes. The second will be to try to give nonjudgmental feedback to the children during problem-solving sessions. That will be more difficult and will require lots of practice. I like to smile and nod my head, though not necessarily in that order.

As the institute drew to a close, Jill's enthusiasm remained high. Since she had enrolled in the ELM (Educational Leaders in Mathematics) component of the program, which was funded by the National

Science Foundation (funding that also paid her tuition to the institute), she would be receiving a mentor/resource person to help her during the year. Because I would be serving in that role, we met briefly at the end of the institute to discuss my visits and to schedule a first meeting in September.

A DESCRIPTION OF THE MENTORING MODEL

According to Jackson (1985), although various models of the mentor/protégé relationship have been advanced, most stem from the mimetic tradition. The mentor is perceived as having all the answers and thus her or his role is to give them to the protégé. The mentor models and tells; the protégé imitates and practices as the mentor encourages and provides corrective feedback. For example, Gray and Gray (1985) propose a five-tiered "helping-relationship" model from a synthesis of the research on mentoring. At levels 1 and 2, they suggest the mentor demonstrate and tell. Level 3 acknowledges the protégé's developing competencies and thus the mentor is encouraged to allow more active problem solving on the part of the protégé. At level 4 the mentor supports the protégé's attempts to try his or her own ideas; whereas at level 5 a now competent protégé is able to function without the help of the mentor. Knowledge, from this perspective, is considered identifiable, objective, and able to be transmitted directly from mentor to protégé.

In contrast to the mimetic tradition, Jackson (1985) proposes the mentor/protégé relationship be characterized by transformation, whereby people's thinking and values are changed as a result of qualitative shifts in their perspectives. Knowledge from this perspective is construed as personal and subjective, albeit socially agreed upon. Grennon (1987) provides this description:

> Mentoring, in this tradition, becomes a process in which the mentor seeks to understand and expand the protégé's present conceptions and ideas from the outset of the relationship. Rather than the protégé seeking to model the behaviors of the mentor, the mentor and the protégé both seek to understand one another's behaviors and proceed from this common understanding. Transformations occur when individuals construct for themselves new relationships, new understandings, or new ways of thinking. Often, the new thinking is triggered by a mentor or protégé asking the "right" question or orchestrating the "right" experience. The learning, however, is constructed by the learner. [pp. 45–46]

The transformation model, as described by Jackson (1985) and Grennon (1987), aligns well with the criteria of phronesis and constructivism delineated in Chapter 2. "Correct" practice is viewed as illusory, and thus knowledge becomes grounded in a "community of discourse," in this case, the community of mentor and protégé as they engage in reflection, conversation, and action. The assimilatory schemes of the protégé in regard to theories about teaching are viewed as the organizing scheme for teaching behavior, with reflection and discussion of contradictions the potent motivator of change. In this way, according to Grennon (1987), the mentor/protégé relationship becomes characterized by four overriding principles:

1. The mentor learns the protégé's point of view through careful listening and probing.
2. The mentor teaches by inquiring at the "leading edge" of the protégé's thinking and by attempting to facilitate "disequilibrium."
3. The mentor constructs a line of *inquiry* meaningful to the mentor, and the protégé constructs a line of *reasoning* meaningful to the protégé. Each partner seeks her or his own meaning while responding to the perceived needs of the other.
4. The mentor acknowledges that the protégé has the intellectual freedom to adopt and modify the pedagogical orientations of her or his choice.

These principles became the bedrock of my work with Jill during the year.

THE YEAR BEGINS

As I drove through the rolling, country hills for my first visit with Jill, I found myself wondering whether the goals Jill had specified in her synthesis paper (to use manipulatives and to provide nonjudgmental feedback during problem-solving sessions) would still be primary to her. A month had lapsed since the institute, and her teaching position had been changed from first grade to second. Since we had planned to meet for the first time during her planning period, in order to discuss my role and a possible schedule for the year, I decided to begin by asking her what had impressed her during the institute and what she would like my help with during the year.

She responded with much enthusiasm. "I just loved it," she exclaimed. "I want to do it all."

I smiled and acknowledged her excitement but then probed for more information. "What do you mean by 'all'?" I asked.

"I want to use open-ended questions, watch my 'wait time,' use manipulatives with problem solving, and teach the kids LOGO." She ended with a flourish, proudly showing me her new Apple computer.

I noted with interest that all her specified goals were procedural or activity based, in contrast to the more conceptual goals of facilitating "invention" or "problem ownership" on the part of learners, or making learning meaningful by starting with the learner's schemes and proceeding from the concrete to the abstract. This beginning point is in line with Meinhard's (Foster & Pellens, 1986) proposition that teacher development proceeds from an initial focus on procedures or behaviors, since they are the observables of the action, to a higher level requiring inferences (beyond the observables) about coordination among the learner, teacher, and subject matter, thus incorporating mutual adjustments. The third level in Meinhard's model requires teachers to understand development and the cognitive connections between the disciplines.

Since this was our first meeting, I made no further comments but agreed to work with Jill toward the accomplishment of her goals. We determined that I would come every Thursday morning for a math period of approximately 45 minutes, with a scheduled conference afterward. (Every Thursday she had a planning period, with lunch directly after, which gave us a long conference/planning time.) I asked her if she would teach a math lesson the following week, so that I might get a sense of her teaching style in order to blend mine with hers. (Although the reason I gave was true, I also wanted to see her "assimilatory scheme" of teaching, in action, so that I could further establish our beginning point.) She agreed, saying that she would lead a problem-solving session, making use of manipulatives.

The following week Jill began her first lesson by writing the number 17 on the chalkboard and asking the children to make up a problem that might have 17 for an answer. Her wait time was excellent; she gave them a great deal of time to think, then accepted answers. The children whom she called on all offered correct solutions, and this seemed to please her. She then distributed a sheet with five word problems (requiring either simple addition or subtraction) and asked the children to work in pairs, using Unifix cubes if they desired. I wandered from pair to pair, listening to the children's reasoning and asking questions. After approximately 15 minutes, even though most of the children had not had time to complete all five problems, Jill asked them to return to their seats to share their solutions as a whole group. Beginning with the first problem as the focus of discussion, she called on a child to explain his solution. Since it was correct, she proceeded to the second problem: If a party began at 4:00 and ended at 8:00, how long did it last? Here there was disagreement. Several children had added and decided the answer was 12; others had subtracted, producing 4. Although Jill did pursue, with questioning, *how* they solved the problem, the children seemed unperturbed by the disagreement and appeared simply to be waiting for her to tell them which solution was correct. She became flustered, did not seem to know where to go with the disagreement, and finally said they would discuss it further tomorrow. She then went on with the remainder of the problems and seemed pleased when correct strategies were offered.

I wanted Jill to see the power of contradiction, so that she would be willing to give counterexamples and heighten disagreements, in order to challenge thinking. I also wanted to expose children's reasoning so that she would see the value in probing for it and using it as a starting base in teaching. We had 10 minutes left in the math period; I asked if I could do a little mental math (Kamii, 1985, 1989) with the class. She agreed.

I wrote 5+8 on the chalkboard and asked the children to think of all the different ways they could to get the answer. After allowing for wait time, I probed for the various strategies used. Patrick explained that he had "counted on from 5." I asked him how he knew to stop at 13, and he explained that his fingers helped; he used 8 of them and stopped after the last.

Ava nodded her head in agreement with Patrick. "I did it that way, too, Patrick," she declared. "Only I began with the 8 and used 5 fingers. It's shorter that way."

Here was an opportunity for a counterexample that would heighten the discussion and probe for conceptual understanding. "But that's a different problem, isn't it? Isn't that 8 plus 5?" I countered.

"But it's the same," Ava declared, adamantly.

"Can you prove that to us?" I knew my request would challenge her, so for support I added, "What a neat shortcut that will be, Ava, if your way will always work." I looked at Patrick. He was intrigued.

Ava thought for a minute, then came to the board and drew a row of 13 lines. Proceeding left to right she circled the first 5, and explained that 5 lines were in the circle and 8 were left. She then circled similarly 5 and 8, moving right to left. "See," she said. "It's like taking 3 from the 8 to make 5 into 8. That makes the 8 into a 5."

The class was getting excited. A third child, Kirk, raised his hand and began, "My way is kind of like your way, Ava — what you just drew, I mean — but it's different from Patrick's. I knew that 8 plus 5 is 13 because 7 plus 6 equals 13."

"How did that help you?" I probed, looking puzzled and feigning ignorance.

"Well, I took 1 off the 8 to make 7, then I added it to the 5 to make 6. I knew 7 plus 6 equals 13, so I didn't need to use my fingers," Kirk proudly declared.

"Hey, I just figured out an even shorter shortcut," piped up another child, Jim, who could not contain his excitement. "Take 2 from the 5 and put it on the 8. That makes 10, and 10 plus 3 is easy." Several hands were up now, and the children were obviously very engaged; but time had run out, and we had to get the class to gym. Jill dismissed them and we began our conference.

Jill opened the conference with obvious enthusiasm over the reasoning she had observed in the children. "I didn't know Kirk could think that way," she exclaimed with surprise in her voice. I acknowledged her enthusiasm and was going to ask what she had noticed that I did to facilitate the thinking, but I didn't need to. As I would discover throughout the year, Jill was an astute observer and placed high value on mathematical reasoning. She went on, "And I love the way you played the 'devil's advocate.' It really made them think more. I can't wait to try it; it will be such fun."

Because I wanted Jill to reflect on the importance of contradiction in the discussion on the second problem, which she had abandoned, I switched the focus by asking her why she had decided to stop the discussion on the problem and move on. She explained that she hadn't known what to do. While she knew that she shouldn't give them the answer, since that would most likely stop their thinking, she believed that the children seemed unaware of the inherent contradiction in the solutions offered. I agreed with her observation, and then we brainstormed together ways to make apparent contradictions more obvious, finally deciding to have the group share solutions in a circle on the rug so that children could demonstrate their solutions with the manipulatives they had used, rather than verbally, and to ask them to try to convince each other that they were right. We also discussed the need to check for understanding by asking volunteers to paraphrase solutions offered and to highlight the arguments.

Last, I asked Jill if she thought the children had had enough time to work through the five problems on the sheet. She explained that she knew they hadn't but had been afraid some would finish too soon. We discussed the benefits of spending time on problems and thinking about alternative solutions. She decided that she would give fewer problems but ask children to find as many different ways to solve them as they could.

During the next several weeks, Jill's enthusiasm grew. The children were becoming accustomed to having to prove their reasoning, and Jill was truly enjoying "playing ignorant" and providing counterexamples to make them do so. She usually planned pair problem-solving sessions using Unifix cubes coupled with mental math, as she had seen me do, for teaching place value. For example, one day when I came in, the children were attempting to figure out $14 + 15$. Some wonderful thinking was going on, with various strategies being shared by the children, such as pretending the 14 was 15, then adding $15 + 15 = 30$, then taking the 1 off to get 29.

One of the children offered a strategy (double-digit addition), which her older brother had showed her. "Add 4 plus 5," she explained, "and you get 9. Then add 1 plus 1 and you get 2. That makes 29."

Jill demonstrated her ability to probe with counterexamples by responding, "But I'm confused, Janine. Nine plus 2 equals 11. How did you get 29?" Jill had succeeded in facilitating disequilibrium. Janine was puzzled. The class also was puzzled over Janine's dilemma.

Finally, one of the children offered a resolution. "I think it works," Jim offered tentatively, "because those are not really ones that Janine added; they are tens. *Ten* plus 4 equals 14; 10 plus 5 equals 15. Those are 2 tens." Place value was beginning to be constructed; the discussion continued.

During our conference, Jill expressed excitement over Jim's discovery and went on to report how she never used the book any more, but instead planned according to what happened each day and what she thought the children needed. She exclaimed of this approach to the teaching of math, "It's the most exciting thing I've ever tried as a teacher." Yet, although Jill *reported* planning and adjusting her teaching in relation to the needs of the learner (and in many respects she did do so), as the weeks wore on I began to suspect she was enamored with her new style and "the approach" and that I needed to challenge her to look more closely at the learner. She seemed to need to decenter from herself and "the working procedures" and focus on the learner in relation to concept development. I suspected this for a couple of reasons. First, Jill had been to an inservice workshop toward the end of October and had come back asking me to challenge her.

"What do you mean," I asked. "How do you want to be challenged?"

"Well, I want to learn about some new materials," she replied, "like logic blocks, or classification games, or chip trading."

"Why?" I asked.

"Because I want the challenge," she responded with circuitous logic.

"How will the materials help the children?" I asked, hoping the question would cause some reflection and a refocus on the needs of the learner.

She was not at all perturbed by my question, but instead responded quickly, "I would like to do some classification activities with them. The blocks would be a good way, wouldn't they?" Although she had analyzed the materials and their potential well, she was making a curriculum decision based on her needs and interests rather than the conceptual needs of the learner.

I had also noticed that, during mental math, about five of the children appeared lost. The numbers had gotten larger (e.g., $32+19$), and a few of the children could not follow the verbal reasoning that many of the others were using to explain regrouping. It seemed apparent to me that Jill had gone about as far as she could with mental math in teaching regrouping and that she needed to make manipulatives available during the activity. Then, when children explained their strategies regarding the parts they were grouping, the use of concrete materials would allow everyone to check the strategy. I had questioned Jill several times about whether she thought all the children were following the discussion, and she had conceded that some were not. But, each time she had simply excused those children as being "slower" or "having a bad day," without considering any modifications she might make in her instruction.

A TRANSFORMATION OCCURS

Shifting to the Learner

I decided to be direct. The next week when we conferred, I specifically focused our discussion on three children who I knew were lost during the mental math activity. "I'm concerned about Patrick, Jessie, and Jeanne," I began. "Do you think that they understood the strategies the other children were describing?"

Jill admitted that they probably had not.

"Do you think they will develop an understanding of regrouping via the mental math approach?" I probed further.

Jill was quiet, obviously reflecting. I had hoped my line of questioning would create disequilibrium, since I knew Jill's assimilatory scheme was that mental math (using counterexamples and probing questions) was a powerful technique. By focusing her on specific learners and their needs, I hoped to create a contradiction whereby she would have to analyze and coordinate the technique *in relation to* the learners' needs. My questioning appeared to be successful.

"I thought so at first," Jill responded pensively, "but I'm not sure now. In the beginning they really seemed to understand, and the approach felt so natural."

"What was different about the task when you began, in contrast to now?" I inquired, pushing her to analyze the learners' needs further.

"I think they could visualize smaller numbers like 18 without manipulatives," she responded after some thought, "but they have no concept of 38, or 72. I'm not even sure they understand that 72 is 7 tens plus 2 ones. Maybe they need more manipulative experience." Jill was beginning to think about instruction conceptually, and in relation to the learner. I concurred with her analysis and then invited her to brainstorm with me ways to adapt the mental math activity to meet the needs of Jeanne, Jessie, and Patrick.

During the next several weeks, Jill showed evidence of her transformation. She continued episodes of mental math, encouraging children to take apart the numbers and regroup them in various ways, but she had the children share their ideas in a circle, using a large cardboard set of base-10 blocks that she had made. She also lengthened the problem-solving sessions, giving the children more time to manipulate numbers concretely in small groups, using Unifix cubes to solve the problems.

One day in November when I came in, she and the children were obviously excited. Jill explained that several children had come up with some theories that they were all currently involved in trying to prove. She had written the theories on the board: Two even numbers added together make an even number; two odd numbers added together make an even number; an odd number divided by an odd number makes an even number; and an odd number plus an even number gives an odd number. The children were working together in groups of threes or fours, using Unifix cubes, attempting to prove or disprove their theories. I wandered from group to group, listening to the children's reasoning. Most of them were approaching the task by trying out several numbers; I suggested they make a record of the numbers they had tried and then look for patterns.

At conference time Jill explained how the investigation had begun. During a mental math activity, some of the children had grouped by twos in order to count more quickly and had found that, while some numbers could be grouped by twos evenly, others had an extra cube left over. Using their experience as a base, Jill had labeled the numbers even and odd. Then they had gone on to investigate what happened when the numbers were added. I shared my enthusiasm with Jill over her willingness to capitalize on the children's experience, as well as to diverge from the work she was doing on place value, to allow for investigation and invention on the part of the learner. We discussed the value of investigating even "wrong" theories, such as the third one, and I shared with her the classic article by Karmiloff-Smith and Inhelder (1974), entitled, "If You Want to Get Ahead, Get a Theory."

Solidifying the Shift

Math Journal Writing.   Because I wanted her to continue focusing on the learner, as she was then doing, and because I thought it would be beneficial for the children to record their theories and proofs about mathematics, I suggested Jill begin math journals with the children. She was already using journal writing in language arts, and so the children were accustomed to writing independently without concern for spelling and to having her write comments back. She loved the idea and agreed to start the next day by having the children record their proofs regarding their theories on odd and even numbers.

During the next several weeks, the math journals became an integral part of Jill's program and were highly successful for both Jill and the children, even more so than I had anticipated at the time of my suggestion. In December, I proposed that Jill write an article explaining how she was using the journals, for publication in *The Constructivist*, the newsletter of the Association for Constructivist Teaching, of which I serve as editor. Jill agreed, and the article was published in the winter edition, resulting in letters from various teachers, one of whom even traveled from as far away as Pennsylvania to see Jill's program in action. Excerpts from her article are included here, to illustrate not only the way in which Jill used the journals but her assimilatory schemes of teaching at the time:

> Currently I am teaching grade two. The children are seven and eight years old and have a wide range of ability levels. With the guidance of the Summermath for Teachers program at Mount Holyoke College, I am implementing a math program in which the children are "reinventing" math. While I have been quite sure that the children are developing understandings and problem solving techniques that will be of value throughout their lives, I have had nothing concrete to reinforce my theory. . . . At the suggestion of my consultant from the Summermath program, a math journal was introduced to the children. Our intent was that this would become a vehicle for the children to record their theories and their information in order to prove or disprove their theories. Rather than having the focus be only suc-

cessful answers, we hoped to emphasize the thinking process behind the answers. However, it turned out to be an even more valuable tool. A truly individualized, constructivistic math program has evolved. The journal entries . . . indicate the facility and comfort with which many of the children are manipulating numbers. They are capable of computing and proving their answers long before they are familiar with the algorithm. In fact, they are constructing their own algorithms and theories. [Lester, 1987, p. 1]

Jill went on describing her process for using the journal, then offered examples of children's entries showing evidence of their thinking. (She corrected the children's spelling, for purposes of readability.)

CHILD 1:   35+16. What I did. I took the 35 and I subtracted 5 from it and made 30. Then I subtracted 6 from the 16 and made 10. Then I added the 10 to the 30 and made 40. Then I added the 5 and the 6 and made 51.

CHILD 2:   35+16=51. I took the thirty-five and made it thirty. Then I took the sixteen and made it ten. Then I added the thirty and the ten together and got forty. Then I added the five from the thirty five and the six from the sixteen and got eleven. I made the eleven a ten. I added the ten to the forty and got fifty. Then I added the one from the eleven and got fifty-one.

CHILD 3:   I know why if you add an odd number to an odd number you get an even number. Say you were adding five plus five. Well you could take one off each top. You would have twelve with six plus six. I want to find out more. [Lester, 1987, p. 2]

Jill also provided an example of the dialogue that occurs between child and teacher as they both make entries (Lester, 1987, pp. 3–4):

In these entries, which span several days, the child and the teacher participate in a written dialogue. Through this dialogue, the child learns to put the knowledge that she has developed about place value into use:

CHILD: 35+16=51. Well, what I did was I added the tens. Then the ones. The 11 I regrouped. I regrouped its ten to the tens place and I got 51. [See Figure 6.1.]

TEACHER: Why did you add the tens first?

CHILD: I did the ones first.

TEACHER: Why did you work with the ones first?

CHILD: That's what I was told to do in first grade. I knew it in second grade because we do mental math. And when we do mental math we add the ones first because it is faster. When we regroup, we need to.

Figure 6.1.   35+16=51.

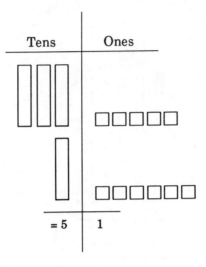

TEACHER: I understand a little better now. What happens when you add 46+25?

CHILD: I am learning a lot of math in second grade. I really like mental math. Now I know a lot more. And it is easier and more fun.

TEACHER: You are thinking a lot. Please try to add 46+25. Draw a picture and explain.

CHILD: 46+25=71. What I did was I got the 46 and added the 25. I added the ones first and then I regrouped. And then the tens. I got 71. [See Figure 6.2.]

By using the journals, Jill had found a way to adapt the mental math activity to meet the needs of her learners. By starting with the learner's assimilatory scheme, evident in the journal entry, Jill could tailor her probing questions to each child's needs and assess and plan her instruction via their understanding. No longer was constructivist teaching merely a "style"; it had become an evolving process based on the learner's needs. Jill concluded,

The addition of a journal component to my math program has served several purposes. The journals have proven to be both a reflection of the child's feelings and a reflection of his/her understanding. Through the journal, the child is receiving individualized 'instruction' and the teacher has an invaluable tool for assessing the child's progress and

Figure 6.2.   46+25=71.

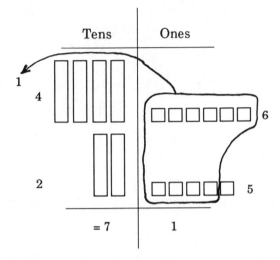

needs. Secondly, the math writing time has fostered a reflection on the process and logic of mathematical reasoning. . . . I believe the journal writing encourages this process. For some children, in fact, the journal might be just the link that makes the discovery of math meaningful. [Lester, 1987, p. 7]

Teaching Geometry.   With journal writing well under way, Jill also began to use the journals as a place for children to record the programs they were writing in LOGO. We had begun LOGO in September by simply giving the children drawing tasks, such as making a square, a triangle, a house, and so forth. By November they were doing simple programming to make the turtle draw a square, such as the following:

> To square
> FD 40 RT 90 FD 40 RT 90 FD 40 RT 90 FD 40
> END

Figure 6.3 shows the path the turtle makes when this program is typed into the computer.

Since Jill by this time clearly had an assimilatory scheme for teaching based on the learner's needs in relation to conceptual development, I shared with her the research on LOGO suggesting that it is debatable whether the procedures used (Forward, right 90, etc.) always transfer to

Figure 6.3. Using a LOGO program to draw a square.

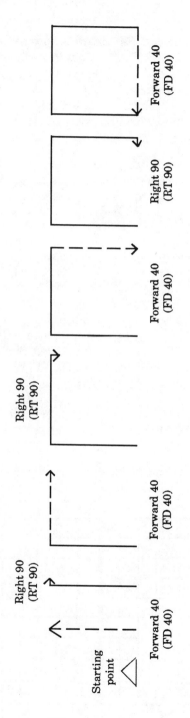

geometric concepts. Jill asked me to teach a lesson so that we might explore together whether this was indeed the case.

The following week I brought graph paper on which several rectangles were outlined (1×6; 6×1; 2×3; 3×2; 2×4) drawn to approximately ten times the size of LOGO shapes. After breaking the class up into small cooperative learning groups, I asked each group to talk together and decide

1. What the LOGO program would be to draw each shape given
2. What the total distance around each shape was
3. How many squares were inside each shape
4. What patterns they noticed and why they thought they happened

My goals were to expose any misconceptions the children might have in transferring LOGO to grid paper, and then, if none existed, to have an open-ended enough task to encourage an investigation into perimeter and area.

Several misconceptions immediately showed up. For the rectangle shown in Figure 6.4, two groups began with the command FD 7, instead of FD 6, because they counted the step the figure began on. Another group wrote FD 6, RT 90, FD 10 (instead of 1), commenting, "It *looks* about as long as FD 10." (They were correct in judging (1 : 10) the visual distance, yet they had used a measurement system based on one unit for each line for the FD 6. Thus, they were inconsistent.) In an attempt to highlight their inconsistency, I commented that FD 6 was

Figure 6.4.   Using a shape drawn on graph paper for creating a LOGO program.

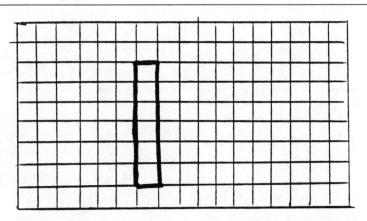

longer than FD 10. They were undaunted and explained that RT 90 made it longer! A heated debate ensued among the children and, unfortunately, gym time came before we reached a resolution.

When Jill and I conferred after the lesson, she was grinning, and began with a comment that showed evidence of her assimilatory scheme being solidly based on the learner: "Well, there's at least a week's worth of lessons there!" We laughed together and began to plan activities based on the children's misconceptions, with the main lead coming from Jill. She suggested that she continue the debate a while longer following lunch, after which she would program the computer so that 10 steps would equal 1. Such an if/then statement would make the size of the shapes on the computer the same as on the graph paper. The children could then test out their programs, producing visible contradictions that would need to be resolved. When I left school that day, I recorded the following notes:

> Jill has made such growth. She can now visualize where to go, given the lack of understanding in the children. She analyzes their errors in order to understand their assimilatory schemes and then plans by trying to facilitate disequilibrium."

A SECOND TRANSFORMATION

Integration Across the Curriculum

As the year wore on, Jill's enthusiasm grew and she began to talk about other subject areas, as well as math, during our conferences. At first she simply asked me for references on how to encourage writing so that children would feel "empowered" as writers. I brought her several of my books on "writing as process" (e.g., Calkins, 1986; Graves, 1983; Henderson, 1985). Since she was already incorporating journal writing as part of her language arts program, we began there. She shared the children's journals with me, and we analyzed them in relation to the writing and spelling stages outlined in the reference books I had shared with her (also discussed in Chapter 4 of this book). By starting from an analysis of the learner's schemes regarding spelling and writing, Jill could then plan appropriate activities.

She also decided to integrate her social studies and science time so that she would have a large block of time for children to work on projects in those areas. Sharing this idea with me one day, she explained how she knew what she wanted to accomplish but was a little unsure as to how to begin. I asked her to tell me what it was she wanted to accomplish.

"I know I want the children actively investigating," she began. "I want them figuring things out, just like they do in math, and then sharing and debating their theories. I want to start with what they know and have them raise questions and problems that they want to solve."

"Sounds like you've answered your own question," I challenged, with a smile.

"What do you mean?" she said quizzically.

"Why not do exactly as you just described?" I responded. "Choose a broad topic for discussion, probe to find out what the children know and want to know, then break them into cooperative research groups and have them design experiments to answer their own questions. You can be the facilitator, helping them find reference material they can read and helping them set up their experiments."

Jill broke into a large grin. "Of course," she exclaimed, "it's so simple!" Pensively, she offered, "You know, teaching is so different for me now. I used to view teaching as being ways of structuring experiences both to motivate the kids and to get individual concepts across successfully. What *I* did was the focus. . . . Now I see teaching as inherently interwoven with the process of learning; the subjects are related because learning is an integrated process."

Deepening Cognitive Connections

Jill was beginning to make a new leap. Having shifted her focus once already from her own actions to the learner, she was now beginning to analyze learning in depth and make connections across disciplines. I decided to try to solidify this new scheme by encouraging her, through questioning, to take a microanalytical view of learning in relation to cognitive development. My hope was that a cognitive perspective would form a framework for connections across disciplines.

My chance to do so occurred a few weeks later. When I entered the classroom, Jill had a problem on the board and the children were working with Unifix cubes in small groups. The problem was, Add 6 to me, then take away 3. You will have 11. What am I? After the children had spent time in groups on the problem, Jill asked the class to join her in a circle on the rug for a sharing of solutions. When she asked for their answers, three were given: 3, 8, and 9. Katy's group had proposed the answer of 3; Jill asked them to share their strategy first. Katy explained that they had taken 6 and subtracted 3. Another child, Kirk, asked her with a puzzled look why she had started with 6 and pointed out that the 6 had to be added to a number. Katy asked Kirk to explain. He took 8 cubes, added them to 6, then subtracted 3 and produced 11. Several children inquired as to how he knew to start with 8. Kirk replied that he hadn't, he had tried various numbers, one of which was 9. He had discovered that 9 was one over so he knew it had to be 8.

Jill asked if anyone could think of a way to get the answer more efficiently, besides just trying various numbers until one worked. After much thought, Ava offered the following explanation: "If you regroup the 8 with two from the 6 you get 10," she began tentatively. "Now take 3 away and you have 11 left," she concluded with a flair.

"That's true, Ava," several children responded with exasperation in their voices, "but you still started with 8. How did you know to do that? That's the question!" Ava admitted she didn't know, and everyone else was indeed also perplexed.

At conference time, Jill shared her surprise at the difficulty of the problem for the children. In order to enable her to analyze the task in relation to the cognition it required, I asked her first how she had expected the children to solve the problem. In response she explained that she had assumed some might start with 11, subtract 6, and add 3.

"All right, now let's look at what they did and what that tells us about their thinking," I went on.

"Well, none of the children had a systematic approach to the problem," Jill began. "They simply used a trial-and-error approach." I agreed and then suggested that we dig even deeper.

After some thought, she offered, "No one seemed able to use 11 as a starting point. They all proceeded by operating on the number in a straightforward way, using the exact operations specified in the problem."

"How is your solution different from theirs?" I probed further.

She responded with assuredness, "I went backwards. I started at the endpoint and reversed every operation. When the problem said 'subtract,' I added. When it said, 'add,' I subtracted."

"And how did you know that would work?" I countered.

Jill was enjoying the challenge. "Because I knew those procedures would reverse what the problem said had been done and that would bring me to my starting point," she concluded with a grin.

Since Jill had isolated and described the reversibility inherently required for a systematic solution to the task, I explained that Piaget (1977) had proposed that reversible thinking was the hallmark of concrete operations. Then, I went on to describe how a stable concrete-operational understanding of a change, or transformation, requires one to understand how to undo, or reverse, the change, given the compensations involved.

Jill was quiet, obviously mulling over Piaget's work, then commented in explanation, "I was thinking about a problem we worked on the other day. I told the children that I had 24 pencils and that I wanted to give one to every child in the class—18. I asked them to figure out how many I would have left. Although they all solved the problem successfully, they argued about whether they had subtracted or added. Those who were 'adding on' to get to 24 were seeing it as an adding problem; others understood the connection between starting at 24 and subtracting 18. Those children who made the connection were using reversible thinking." I agreed with Jill's analysis, and we began to discuss tasks in language arts and science that also require reversible thinking.

During the next several weeks I noted with interest that Jill's problem-solving sessions often revolved around problems that enabled her to analyze children's logic. For example, one March day Jill decided to begin some work with the children on patterning. I was late for the math period, having been detained by a student in my office, and the lesson was nearing a close when I arrived. We began our conference with Jill explaining that she had shown the children four different pattern blocks: a square, a triangle, a hexagon, and a quadrilateral and asked them to arrange them in as many ordered patterns as they could. I asked her what strategies she had observed the children using. She replied that, although she had been interested to see if anyone would control the variables and systematically order them into all possible permutations, everyone so far was approaching the problem through a trial-and-error fashion, simply making an arrangement, then checking to see if they had made that arrangement yet. I explained that, while I found her problem interesting, I seriously doubted that any second graders would be able to conclude with logical necessity that they had found all possible permutations, since that type of thinking, according to Piaget, was not usually constructed until around the age of 13 (Wadsworth, 1978).

Jill disagreed. "No, I think Piaget is wrong," she declared. "I'm convinced that some of my children will eventually solve the problem systematically. I've been amazed lately at what I've seen them doing." She paused, thinking back on the lesson. "I may have started with too difficult a problem, though, and so when they've had a chance to share their solutions to this one, I'm going to give them a problem with only three items." Although I disagreed with Jill's prediction, I thought it was important to let the activity continue so that we could further analyze the children's reasoning.

To my surprise, when I returned the following week, Jill asked Patrick to show me his journal entry explaining his solution to a three-item problem. Patrick timidly handed me his journal, but with an intense pride written on his face. He had drawn the illustration shown in Figure 6.5 and written, "Frist i trid the triangle and the square and i nu there was onle 2 ways. Then i trid 3 shaps and i nu there was 2 ways for each. Then i counted and got 6 ways. i no thats all there is cuz i did them all."

Jill had been correct in her analysis; Patrick, indeed, had proven the problem systematically! "Wow, that's some proof, Patrick," I exclaimed. "You've convinced me that there are no more." Patrick beamed from ear to ear. I looked at Jill and realized that her eyes were glistening with tears. I was so proud of her; she had forged ahead, even in the face of challenge from me and long-standing research contradicting her theory. Trusting in her own analysis of the children's cognitive ability, she had given them the opportunity to investigate and construct. She was empowered, and she had succeeded in empowering the children. The note she wrote to me at the end of the year attests to this empowerment:

Thank you for being there and encouraging me throughout the year. With your guidance, I was able to fly.

A "COMMUNITY OF DISCOURSE" BEGINS IN THE SCHOOL

As Jill's enthusiasm grew during the year, it was no longer contained only within the walls of her classroom. She began to invite other teachers from the school into her room so that they might share in her excitement. Because the school was a small one, typical of many of the Berkshire hill-town schools, there was only one teacher per grade and

Figure 6.5. Patrick's proof.

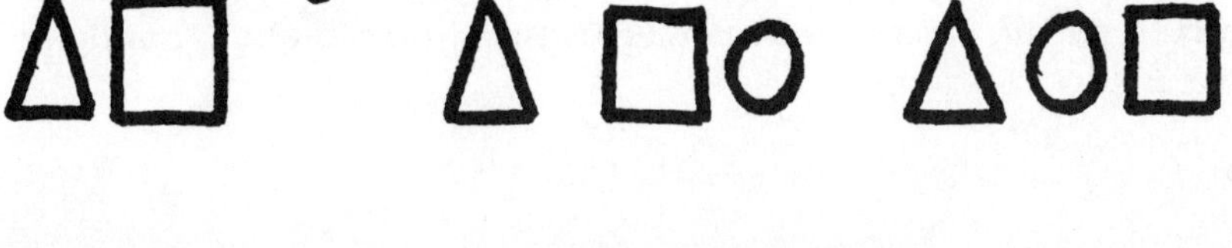

the teachers were a closely knit group. This atmosphere lent itself well to the establishment of a "community of discourse."

The teachers who visited Jill's math period quickly realized that something very special was happening, and they began to use Jill as a resource. They invited her into their classrooms to do demonstration math lessons with their children and frequently sought her out for advice on how to teach certain concepts and on what materials to use. Even the speech and language teacher became involved. She had visited Jill's class and had been astounded at the language development she observed as the children debated theories and explained their reasoning to each other, and so she had become a frequent visitor and participant in discussions.

One day, Ginny, the third-grade teacher next door to Jill, asked if she might join us for lunch on the day of my scheduled visit. When we met, Ginny explained that she was beginning double-digit multiplication with her group, and while she had been trying to use manipulatives (base-10 blocks) with Jill's encouragement, she was struggling with how to show multiplication with the rods. I shared several different activities that I had done in the past with children and then suggested that she might want to "play around" with the rods herself to find various ways to represent multiplication. Ginny, however, did not seem very intent on seeking solutions to her question, and then I began to realize the real mission of our luncheon when she ventured, "Jill's been encouraging me to take the Summermath program next year, but to be honest I'm very nervous about having someone in my room once a week."

"Why?" I asked.

"I don't feel comfortable being observed," she replied.

I knew she needed reassurance about my role. "Ginny, my role is not to observe and evaluate, nor even to critique, unless you ask me for that. My role is simply to be a resource during the year to help you implement whatever it is that *you* want to implement," I responded with what I hoped she would see as warm encouragement and acceptance of her goals. She visibly relaxed and said that she would continue to think about it. Several weeks later she met me in the hall and commented that she and another teacher from the school had both applied for the next summer.

With two other teachers in the program, during the following school year Jill's role as resource continued, and she offered several inservice workshops for teachers in the district as well as a workshop for parents. In 1988–1989, three of the teachers in the district, along with Jill, prepared to offer a series of four inservice workshops for the district. And Jill, Ginny, and another teacher, Joanne, are currently involved in a research project with me to validate the learning that we know is occurring.

As the program began to spread, a group of teachers (three from Jill's school and three others within the district) began to meet on a steady basis to discuss planning, analyze the reasoning of children that they were observing, and support each other as change was made. They hold as their goals reflection, discourse, and action.

7

Branching Out:
The Spread of Green Ideas

Have you ever considered how complicated things can get,
what with one thing leading to another?
— E. B. White, *Charlotte's Web*

In his classic children's book, *Charlotte's Web*, E. B. White (1952)
satirically illustrates how humans are prone to seeing only the particu-
lars of a situation and often miss the whole. Charlotte, a kind and wise
spider, comments, "If I can fool a bug, I can surely fool a man. People
are not as smart as bugs" (p. 67). She then saves her friend Wilbur, a pig,
from slaughter by writing the words "Some pig!" into her web. As she
suspects, the humans focus on the words, take them as fact, and utterly
deny the possibility that they were written by a spider. Dialogue between the farmer and the family physician further illustrates the satire:

"Do you understand how there could be any writing in a spider's
web?"
"Oh, no," said Dr. Dorian. "I don't understand it. But for that
matter I don't understand how a spider learned to spin a web in the
first place. When the words appeared, everyone said they were a
miracle. But nobody pointed out that the web itself is a miracle." [p.
109]

This quote, illustrating the tendency of our species to dig deeper
and deeper, while often missing the whole, was the topic of discussion
around my dinner table the other night. A friend of mine, who is a
landscaper, shared what I thought was a wonderful analogy.
"It's like when landscapers set out to plant a row of trees," he
explained, "with each shovel full of dirt your hole seems more wonderful; and the deeper you go, the more wonderful it becomes. If you go
too deep, though, you lose your ability to communicate with the other
landscapers around you. You may all have succeeded in digging wonder-

ful holes, but if you're too deep, no one can communicate to let the others know where he is."

This tendency to dig deeper often results, in academia, in narrow perceptions and a lack of communication across disciplines. In contrast, understanding the disciplines simply as human, arbitrary categories of information is liberating. Although the traditional disciplines may have served to organize knowledge efficiently and make communicating easier in the past, as new information emerges unbinding these old categories, new doors may be opened that are more helpful in solving general problems of the real world. It is the intent of this chapter, first, to unbind old categories and, then, to look at the disciplines in a new light in relation to teacher-education programs.

A CASE FOR INTERDISCIPLINARY THOUGHT

Breadth Versus Depth in Research

There are at least three reasons why interdisciplinary research is currently needed and why a trend in that direction is beginning to occur: (1) a focus on real-world problems, (2) a rise in technology, and (3) the increase of abstract methodologies within disciplines (Winkler, 1987).

Real-World Problems.   Few if any "real-world problems" fit into the jurisdiction of single disciplines alone. For example, although we have a great deal of information, via various disciplines, about our cities, we have yet to get it all together to make them livable. The threat of nuclear war has brought together scholars who study climate, population patterns, the history of past disasters, as well as philosophers interested in ethics and moral philosophy. And AIDS research involves epidemiologists, molecular biologists (a field which itself is a combination of physics and biology), and chemists, as well as lawyers, politicians, and activists involved in human rights issues. In the social sciences, the rise of the modern welfare state in the second half of the twentieth century brought together history, political science, economics, philosophy, and law, in a debate on the limits and obligations of the authority of government. In fact, driven by a growing conviction that important questions about nature and society can no longer be neatly divided among the traditional disciplines, scholars, in general, are crossing disciplines and seeking funding together. The National Science Foundation, for example, has recently appropriated money for several new multidisciplinary engineering research centers (Winkler, 1987).

New Technologies.   In the last few decades, as technological advances have been made, new questions for researchers have arisen and new tools have become available. In some cases boundaries between disciplines have been merely muddied; in others, new disciplines have evolved. Computer technology, for instance, served as the impetus in the development of the field of artificial intelligence and, in so doing, united mathematicians, psychologists, and linguists. Later expansion under the more general rubric of cognitive science involved scholars in neuroscience, anthropology, and philosophy as well (Gardner, 1985). Biotechnology, a rising multimillion-dollar industry that biologically synthesizes products ranging from insulin to artificial sweetener, merged biology and chemistry. Even education was not left alone. The rise in technology brought new media, such as video, television, opaque and transparent projectors, as well as computers, to the general market. Many educators began to have more in common with the fields of graphics, communications, psychology, and business and industry, and eventually the field of educational technology was formed.

Abstract Methodologies.   Perhaps the most interesting observable case in what Geertz (1980) has called "blurred genres" is the way in which researchers have begun to look at "how they think about how they think." As the full effect of the realization of the problem of being both observer and participant in what is being studied began to hit the academic community, many scholars began to focus on not only what *questions* they might ask but on *how* those questions might be asked. In Geertz's words, "Individuals thinking of themselves as social (or behavioral or human or cultural) scientists became free to shape their work in terms of its necessities rather than received ideas as to what they ought or ought not to be doing" (p. 167). As the methodologies used in the research became the focus, many scholars began to find more in common with others using the same methodologies, rather than (as in the past) with scholars in their own field.

Structuralism, for example, first derived its roots from the mathematical concept of a system with a set of laws and regulations explaining the change of parts within a whole. This notion was extended into the field of linguistics by Chomsky (1957), when sentence structure and "transformational grammar" became the focus; then, it was further extended into biology by Waddington (1975), into psychology by the gestalt group (Koffka, 1935) and by Piaget (1970), and into the social sciences by Durkheim (1954) and Lévi-Strauss (1963).

Textualism, a new methodology that isolates the documents and readings of a field and analyzes them as a focus of study, is currently also serving to bridge disciplines. The bridge appears to be based on an epistemology that criticizes the dominant notion that knowledge can be discovered and that there is a common language of knowing. Winkler (1987) quotes Robert Sholes, director of the interdisciplinary Center for Modern Culture and Media at Brown University:

> I rather think the humanities and some of the social sciences are shrink-
> ing into one large discipline. Divisions between, for example, literature
> and philosophy are not as great as they used to be. It would be very
> easy, if you didn't have all the traditional department names, to put
> together a single department — call it a textual department. [p. A15]

Although many scholars argue about the impact of methodologies such as textualism and structuralism, the fact that methodologies form a core around which scholars congregate is not debatable. Developments in higher mathematics, for example, have united many of the sciences; and anthropology, while it once was based on fieldwork in a classic systems sense, now borrows heavily from history and literary analysis; and schools such as minimalism and abstract impressionism cross the traditional discipline lines of art, music, and literature. Boundaries are becoming nebulous as scholars search for breadth, rather than depth, and many see the reformulation of boundaries as a sign of the refiguration of thought (Geertz, 1980). Gerald Holton, professor of physics and the history of science at Harvard, likens interdisciplinary research to branches on a tree, which, "by growing outwards in different directions . . . enable the tree to grow upward in one direction" (quoted in Winkler, 1987, p. A14).

Breadth Versus Depth in Institutions

Higher Education.   Although it seems obvious that our real-world problems are interdisciplinary and thus interdepartmental, in-terprofessional, and interdependent, our institutions still cling to a heavy bias toward depth rather than breadth. Cleveland (1986) argues that such a bias has been useful in the past; for example, during the scientific and industrial revolutions, the chopping up of the study of physical reality into "vertically sliced puzzles, each to be deciphered separately by a different analytical chain of reasoning (a discipline) made possible the division and specialization of labor" (p. 63). But, as new information comes to the forefront, the traditional divisions be-come less and less helpful.

The bias is still strong, but slowly a new wave of curricular reform, emphasizing interdisciplinary connections for a changing world, is building. Heller (1987), recently reporting for *The Chronicle of Higher Education* on current undergraduate reforms, cites several examples of evolving interdisciplinary programs. Twelve faculty members at St. Vincent College, in the fall of 1988, introduced classic texts in several courses so that students might study the same text from various perspectives. At the University of California at Berkeley, interdisciplinary courses will soon be offered, team taught by three senior scholars; one of the courses is called "Contemporary Issues in Civilization." Even the classic math/science program of the Massachusetts Institute of Technology is under reform, with a widening of the humanities requirements for engineers.

Some colleges have even implemented full programs. For example, Los Medanos College, a two-year school in California, introduced a general curriculum in 1983 in which each course focuses in part on the discipline's "mode of inquiry." Brooklyn College's program, however, is perhaps the most well known, with its new core curriculum boasting course titles such as "People, Power, and Politics" and "Knowledge, Existence, and Values" (Heller, 1987).

Although change is occurring slowly, it has begun. Barriers are falling. In fact, such changes have led Ernest Boyer to state that he has sensed currently "more intense and constructive debate about undergraduate education than in perhaps the last three decades" (quoted in Heller, 1987, p. A28).

Elementary and Secondary Institutions.   A similar but more slowly emerging shift toward interdisciplinary thinking is occurring in our elementary and secondary institutions. The shift on this level is characterized by an emphasis on thinking and a move toward integration of the curriculum.

The focus on thinking is the result of criticism from many directions. Futurists, for example, assail the schools for teaching facts that will be outdated before they are forgotten by the children learning them. They suggest instead that schools teach learners to access, organize, analyze, and synthesize material, which will be available via computers at simply the touch of a fingertip. Cleveland (1986), with the following quip, highlights the futility of teaching facts: "The last time I took physics, I was told the atom couldn't be split—a fact that has not served me well in the nuclear era" (p. 64). He argues instead for teaching general theory that can serve as a framework for the shifting facts students will encounter over a lifetime.

Other critics, like DeBono (1986), claim that schools have approached the teaching of thinking simply by incorporating problem solving or critical thinking, a type of cognition which, itself, is too narrow. He states, "Perhaps the most damaging limitation of thinking is to see only a narrow part of a situation and then to come to a conclusion. It is the error made when we think only in the short term . . . when we think only ego-centrally" (p. 14). Arguing that "just being critical is not nearly enough," he makes a case for teaching what he has termed "lateral thinking," which is more "constructive, generative, and organizing in nature" (p. 13). It involves two basic processes: (1) breadth — making connections or correspondences between various alternatives — and (2) change — making transformations such as viewing the same thing from different perspectives. To date, although change has come slowly in this country, 30 percent of the schools in Great Britain now teach lateral thinking (the term has even been added to the *Oxford English Dictionary*), and Bulgaria and Venezuela have incorporated it in their schools nationwide (DeBono, 1986).

The move toward an integrated curriculum has perhaps been more erratic. Because of pressure to add new topics continually to the curriculum and eventually finding it a physical impossibility due to time constraints, some administrators have begun to encourage teachers to find ways of integrating subject areas. On the surface, the integration may appear to be a "rehash" of the old "core" curriculum notion, but when looked at with more scrutiny it has a distinct contemporary flavor. Students are involved in project work that integrates the traditional disciplines of language arts and mathematics, but in so doing they are learning not only to *solve* problems but to *pose* problems. Rather than teachers deciding on themes of study, students choose areas they would like to research, refine their questions into researchable issues, then spend time accessing information and organizing it for communication to others. Communication takes various forms, from art or music projects to writing reports. In a sense, the process, rather than the product, becomes the curriculum. Students are learning how to learn and to communicate what they have learned to each other.

But, the question looms, Are our teachers equipped to meet these shifting demands?

Breadth Versus Depth for Teachers

Twenty years ago I faced a dilemma common to most undergraduates — choosing a major. Weighing both academic and vocational interests was a sticky issue, in that, for as many doors that opened with one choice, others closed. With academic credits structured as they were, majoring in more than one field (or even fitting in what I deemed to be related courses) in four years was impossible.

Teacher educators, as they design programs for prospective teachers, face the same dilemma today. Most frequently, elementary teachers complete approximately two years of undergraduate liberal arts and then transfer into departments of education to complete a major in education. Secondary teachers, on the other hand, complete a major in an academic discipline, with only a few courses in education, usually a course in educational psychology and/or curriculum and a practicum experience. Upon graduating and entering the work force, elementary teachers have been criticized for their lack of content in the traditional subject areas, whereas secondary teachers have been criticized for an overemphasis on single subjects and a lack of understanding of the child and learning theories.

Current reformers (Carnegie Forum, 1986; Holmes Group, 1986) criticize traditional practice, arguing that a liberal-arts major should be required of all teachers. Indeed, such a movement appears to be afoot nationally, with several states already requiring a liberal-arts degree for certification.

While reform seems to be a primary concern within state boards of education, confusion over the direction it should take reigns. Since 1986, although 32 states have revised their teacher-education curricula, some have mandated a liberal-arts major and decreased the number of professional education courses, while others have taken an opposite tack and increased the amount of pedagogical course work (Leatherman, 1988). The critical issue appears to center around what majors might have more worth in the educating of teachers. For example, it could be argued that philosophy, since it deals with reasoning and knowledge, would be a powerful major in developing thinking teachers. Or that psychology, since it involves the study of human behavior, emotions, and thought processes, might go a long way in developing teachers with keen insights into child development and learning. Others argue that the purpose of the liberal-arts degree is to develop a deeper content base in teachers; thus, they see more value in mathematics, science, or the humanities. These reformers propose that the purpose of the liberal-arts major be for broad general education, and they argue that all such majors are equal, the assumption being that requiring a liberal-arts major will produce a varied pool of educated applicants to the teaching profession. On the surface this perspective appears tenable, yet critics of this viewpoint argue that little value exists for majors such as chemistry or Shakespearean literature for a first-grade teacher.

In order to develop empowered teachers, teachers as researchers, it seems clear that what is needed is a major that opens the mind, broadens awareness, and widens horizons, rather than one that trains for specific career preparation. The major needs to cultivate the intellect and the imagination to develop thinking ability, rather than provide vocational skills. In Murray's (1986) words, "The reform of teacher education must be coupled with changes in the education that undergraduates receive in the arts and sciences. Courses in the core subjects that elaborate both the structure of a discipline and its powerful and generative ideas must be developed" (p. 30). Although it is possible that a liberal-arts major, particularly when it is self-chosen and fulfilling, might engender high-level thinking and open new intellectual doors, an interdisciplinary major may be an even more powerful influencer, if it is carefully designed with that intent. The next section presents a proposal for such an interdisciplinary alternative.

ESTABLISHING A COMMUNITY OF DISCOURSE

In May of its 1986 legislative session, the Connecticut General Assembly passed the Educational Enhancement Act (Connecticut General Assembly, 1986) requiring all certified teachers receiving degrees after 1990 to complete a four-year "subject area curriculum approved by the State Board of Education" (p. 44). The Board of Education defined the legislation, a year later, to include a minimum of 40 semester hours of credit in (1) a single subject, (2) an interdisciplinary major, or (3) a liberal studies major. Further, professional-education courses were specified as being *nonusable* toward the subject-area major.

In the fall of 1986, under the gun of impending legislation, and with concern over the national crisis in teacher education, the Vice President of Academic Affairs at Southern Connecticut State University, Dr. Anthony Pinciaro, established a "think tank" composed of eight faculty members (four from departments of the School of Education and four from departments of the School of Arts and Sciences) and the deans of the two schools, who chaired the group. The purpose of the group was to review the literature on teacher-education programs, as well as the legislation, and to make recommendations as to academic majors that would facilitate the development of "empowered, thinking" teachers. I served as a member of the group, along with Betsy Foye (elementary education), Carolyn Vanacore (physical education), Louise Spear (special education), Michael Shea (English), David Levine (art history), David Marczely (science), Elsa Falls (psychology), Ella Erway (communications, and acting dean of education), and F. E. Lowe (philosophy, and acting dean of arts and sciences).

The atmosphere of the group was one of excitement and interest; the discussions were provocative and heated. After much deliberation, the group recommended (in line with the principles of self-regulation and constructivism outlined earlier) that teachers ought to have the freedom to pursue academic undergraduate majors of their own interest, but we decided, as well, to continue working together to develop a more innovative, interdisciplinary major as an alternative that would be available to all students.

A New Major Is Proposed

A major to include three strands of interdisciplinary thought (the arts and humanities, the social sciences, and the natural sciences) was proposed as a result, with an implementation starting date of fall 1989. The following key concepts were designated as the core of the program:

1. How knowledge is constructed within the strand; that is, how the process of thinking used in forming the knowledge base actually affects the knowledge base.
2. The relationships, connections, and dialectics between the subjects within the strand.
3. Traditional and creative thinking within the strand (a historical approach).
4. Critical and lateral thinking within the strand, including methodologies and resources.
5. General background content in the traditional fields within the strand. For arts and humanities, fields include art, communications, English, foreign languages, journalism, music, philosophy, and theater; for social sciences, fields include geography, economics, history, political science, psychology, and sociology/anthropology; and for natural sciences, they include biology, chemistry, computer science, earth sciences, mathematics, and physics.

All students in the program will take Introduction to Interdisciplinary Thought, the first-level one-semester course, in the sophomore year, after which they will choose one of the three strands as their focus for their junior and senior years. The following outline gives a broad overview of the seven courses that form the core for this major (see Appendix for more detail):

    A. Sophomore year (required course): Introduction to Interdisciplinary Thought
    B. Junior year (select one)
        1. Perspectives in the Arts and Humanities
        2. Perspectives and Interpretations in the Social Sciences
        3. Perspectives on the Nature of Thinking in the Natural Sciences
    C. Senior year (select one, in the same area as junior year)
        1. Seminar in the Arts and Humanities
        2. Seminar in the Social Sciences
        3. Seminar in the Natural Sciences

In addition, over the three-year period, students will take nine more courses in the disciplines within their chosen strand.

Sample Courses

Over the summer of 1987, seven new interdisciplinary courses were developed by the following faculty: David Levine (art history), Michael Shea (English), Harry Haakonsen (science), and Robert Gelbach (political science). I served as a consultant to the group, contributing expertise in psychology and education, and Peter Brancazio, from Brooklyn College's interdisciplinary program, joined us as outside project consultant. To illustrate the content and format of the program, the new courses are described briefly as follows, with the permission of SCSU (see Appendix for more information).

Introduction to Interdisciplinary Thought. Thinking strategies in the arts and humanities, social sciences, and natural sciences are studied by examining a common theme. Methodology and its cultural bias are analyzed. A different theme is the focus each time the course is taught. Sample themes are revolution, certainty, investigation, and creativity. (A general description follows, but a detailed outline for the theme of revolution is included in the Appendix.)

Introduction to Interdisciplinary Thought immerses students in three conceptually related inquiries, one in each strand. Students are invited to consider similarities and differences between and within the strands, and to consider the following questions: Are the strands distinguished by objective differences in their subject matter alone? Do they represent different ways of experiencing the world and/or different forms of inquiry, or simply cultural bias and habit?

Owing to its broad scope, the course is team taught by representatives of the three major areas. Each instructor is the principal lecturer/ discussion leader for one-third of the course, but regular interchange among the participants and all faculty creates a stimulating classroom atmosphere. Emphasis is on demonstrating the value of multiple points of view, rather than on distributing facts to students.

Perspectives in the Arts and Humanities. The course defines and analyzes a series of methods common to disciplines in the arts and humanities, to show how each contributes to understanding objects of study. Each section of the course begins with a reading and discussion of studies that apply one method of interpretation to the work chosen for analysis. Then that same method of analysis is applied to a limited group of works in at least two other disciplines in the strand. The ultimate point of this approach is to show how each methodology contributes something different to understanding an object of study. Although the course examines the critical thinking process in the arts and humanities, it presents neither a comprehensive overview nor a historical survey of critical methods. Rather, it attempts to understand the limits of our knowledge prescribed by a critical method and how this method determines what we know and do not know in artistic and humanistic thought.

Perspectives and Interpretations in the Social Sciences. How do the social sciences "explain"? What makes them "scientific"? These questions are approached by exploring a single theme from different disciplinary perspectives, using several common modes of interpretation. Themes vary each year; topics include work and play, childhood, education, deviance, communication, health and illness, family, religion, and technology. (A detailed outline of the theme of work and play is included in the Appendix.) The purpose of this course is to give a reflective overview of the social science disciplines at work on a common theme, a sampling of the insights diverse disciplines can offer to commonplace social phenomena, and some concrete experiences of how an investigator's mode of explanation and methods of inquiry both facilitate and limit the growth of social knowledge.

While each discipline is commonly thought of as having its "own" subject matter, this course proceeds on the hypothesis that, in fact, the common subject matter of all these disciplines is humans as social beings who interact in meaningful cultural systems. Each discipline investigates and theorizes about some part of these human systems, observing rules of evidence and inference, seeking to "explain" observed phenomena by accounting for them within conceptual models that are consistent with the evidence, and often generating rival theories and models to account for the same phenomena. To exemplify these features of social science, the course focuses on a theme or problem which (1) is found universally in human cultural systems and (2) has been an object of study from several disciplinary perspectives.

Perspectives on the Nature of Thinking in the Natural Sciences.
This course focuses on creative discoveries, ideas, and trends of thought in the natural sciences. It examines the nature of scientific thinking and investigation by comparing and contrasting "scientific" and "nonscientific" ways of viewing the world of ideas. Careful attention is given to the application and interpretation of the "scientific method," in that, throughout the course, students are exposed to a series of "methods of inquiry" common to the various fields of science.

Senior Seminars. A high-level seminar in each of the three strands treats problem posing and solving, resources, and research in the strand by engaging students in interdisciplinary research projects. Faculty and students choose projects together.

IMPLICATIONS

This chapter has presented a case for interdisciplinary thinking and then outlined a proposed interdisciplinary major at SCSU. It has *not* been my intent here to suggest that an interdisciplinary major such as this be required as an inherent aspect of teacher education, although I do believe it is an enticing program. Many other fine programs exist, and assuredly more radical interdisciplinary programs could be proposed. Instead, my intent has been to illustrate one alternative interdisciplinary program that grew out of a "community of discourse," a community of faculty integrating arts and sciences with education.

While the primary purpose of our group was to develop an interdisciplinary major, an interesting side effect occurred. As faculty began discussing the team teaching of interdisciplinary courses, an excitement grew and the traditional barriers between liberal arts and education began to break down. Several faculty members even began to discuss teaching together courses such as those suggested in Chapters 4 and 5. Since our SCSU program is scheduled to go into action in the fall of 1989, as of this writing, there is no dialogue to share evidencing empowerment, as in the previous chapters. Yet setting for inquiry, reflection, and dialogue has been established, and the seeds have been sown.

Criticism of the concept of developing an interdisciplinary major is to be anticipated. Certainly approaches toward developing a general education are not new, and those that criticize teachers' lack of depth in specific disciplines may see this as only another attempt at breadth. It *is* an attempt at breadth, but it is not piecemeal. By fostering deeper understanding of the connections between subject areas, it weaves a powerful web. The web contains not only an understanding of the structures of traditional subjects, but knowledge of their modes of inquiry and epistemology as well.

Since the chapter began with a quote from E. B. White's *Charlotte's Web* (1952), it seems appropriate to end with one:

> A spider's web is stronger than it looks. Although it is made of thin, delicate strands, the web is not easily broken. [p. 55]

8

In Full Bloom

"Come, my beloved,
consider the lilies.
We are of little faith.
We talk too much.
Put your mouthful of words away
and come with me to watch
the lilies open in such a field . . . "

— Anne Sexton, "From the Garden"

The path a seed takes from germination to full bloom is often not an easy one. The soil may be stony, and Mother Nature may not always be bountiful. Hot, scorching suns, too much rain, periods of drought, and competition from weeds all have their effects.

The path of change in teacher education will be no easier. A climate of experimentation and professional autonomy is needed; empowered teachers will need the latitude and authority to develop curricular content, design management strategies, and be involved in determining certification standards. Yet, the current demands for accountability from the state, the community, and industry have produced a drive toward universal curricula and measures of evaluation often at odds with such autonomy and empowerment.

For "full bloom" to be achieved, at least two linkages as introduced in Chapter 2, need to occur: (1) a linkage between liberal-arts and sciences faculty and education faculty and (2) a linkage between the public schools and university education departments. Establishing successful linkages will, at a minimum, be difficult. For example, although many universities currently are beginning to discuss interdisciplinary research, new programming, and team-teaching ventures, the institutional structures that regulate research, particularly university departments, still strongly resist change, and many of the discussions that do occur are taking place in study groups, symposia, conferences, and institutes that are outside of departments (Winkler, 1987). "Turf" battles are still rampant as departments fight over courses and students to establish FTE loads. As young, untenured faculty struggle for recognition and security of position, they usually choose the safer, more creditable avenues of traditional departmental research and activities. Until universities recognize the value of interdisciplinary research, and adjust the workload to enable team teaching and involvement with education faculty, the linkage will be tenuous.

Establishing a linkage with the public school community will also be rife with bumps. Goodlad (1987) compares public-school/university linkages to a "marriage partnership" and explains that successful partnerships have at least three essential characteristics: a degree of dissimilarity between or among the partners, the mutual satisfaction of self-interests, and a measure of selflessness on the part of each sufficient to assure the satisfaction of self-interest by all involved. After several years trying to foster such partnerships, Goodlad concluded that the third characteristic, a measure of selflessness, is often missing. University commitment to public school teachers is often blurred, and, reciprocally, public schools perceive the pursuance of a close school/university relationship as not worth the time and effort.

The obstacles are not insurmountable, but they will demand a great deal of effort and make the way stony and rough. For this reason, radical change may actually be easier to accomplish than incremental change. As the Carnegie Forum report (1986) points out, piecemeal reform simply leaves many teachers, professors, administrators, and school boards frustrated and at odds with each other.

ESTABLISHMENT OF GRADUATE CENTERS

The establishment of graduate centers for teacher education is one such radical change that might lessen some obstacles. These centers, while affiliated with universities, are conceived of as separate entities in themselves and would maintain a degree of autonomy, as do medical schools. Certain public schools would be designated (agreed to by all parties involved) to serve as attached laboratory settings, just as certain hospitals serve as the seat for medical schools. "On-the-cusp" research would be the primary focus and would be engaged in together by teachers, professors, and prospective teachers, all of whom would be graduate students. Innovative practice would be tried, with inservice courses and workshops offered to area teachers for which they may earn credit.

The centers also are perceived of as "think tanks," housing applicable interdisciplinary research and establishing a climate for a community of discourse where liberal-arts and sciences faculty might join education faculty for reflection, conversation, and action. The governing boards would be composed of representatives from the two links, the public school and the university. Thus the links are established right at the start and the need for incentives or coercion to work together is eliminated.

Architecture, medicine, law, audiology, and speech pathology all currently require graduate degrees. Although prelaw or premedicine courses may be taken on an undergraduate level, the final certifying degree is not achieved until the completion of a graduate program. These fields are analogous to education in that they have aspects of many disciplines within them (e.g., architecture requires a working knowledge of design, art history, physics, and mathematics; audiology draws from the physics of sound, language, psychology, and neurology), and as such they can be philosophical or scientific in nature, but they also are based on action, or clinical practice.

A "teacher-as-researcher" model requires teachers to explore the structures of subject matter as well as the content, to be cognizant of the mode of inquiry of the disciplines (how the structures are constructed), and to investigate the processes by which learners "reinvent" the structures of the subjects. Rather than sacrificing one for another, extending the education program to a graduate level allows time for a broad, general education to be developed, as well as a pedagogy of action. Deciding to become a teacher should be a gradual, well-thought-out process. Establishing education as a graduate degree allows for much-needed self-exploration, the development of an understanding of the interdisciplinary nature of learning, and the pursuit of personal academic interests, and it provides time to investigate how learning and thinking are connected to teaching.

Separate centers have been advocated and tried before. For example, some might argue that the "normal school" concept separated teacher education from the mainstream of the university and that, exactly because it was separate, it failed. The proposition put forth here is distinctly different. Normal schools were vocational in nature; graduate centers are professional, and emphasis is placed on research. A teacher-as-researcher model requires inquiry, reflection, and investigation, which are more typically characteristics of graduate education.

Nor is it new to suggest teaching be based on reflection and action. Certainly Dewey advocated such principles as far back as the 1930s. The proposal being advocated, however, extends Dewey's work by adding a graduate-level research base (inquiry on teaching and learning) and by proposing a linkage between the university and the public school system.

The recommendation that teacher-education programs be viewed as professional preparation on the graduate level is also not new. Both the Holmes Group (1986) and the Carnegie Forum (1986) emphatically recommend abolishing undergraduate degrees, and the American Federation of Teachers has supported their proposals (Wiggins, 1986). In fact, several five-year programs already exist. Most, however, suggest graduate programs in order to extend what is being done at present, by adding more pieces, rather than changing the whole. The liberal-arts component is simply lengthened, and vocational training (traditional methods courses and fieldwork) is attached at the end. Instead, radical change is needed. Empowered teaching mandates not only graduate work, but a distinctly different model of education.

INTEGRATING GRADUATE AND UNDERGRADUATE STUDIES

The Undergraduate Program

If teacher-education programs are seated in graduate centers affiliated with universities and are attached to public schools, then undergraduate prospective teachers will be allowed either to pursue their own academic interests or to take a "pre-education" major. This would put their preparation on a par with other professionals such as lawyers and doctors and make them more desirable candidates for acceptance into graduate schools. Such a major might be interdisciplinary in nature and focused on learning and thinking, as was the example presented in the previous chapter.

Interested faculty from the university liberal-arts program would meet with faculty from the education center regularly, forming a community of discourse, the purpose being to discuss alternative ways of teaching the content in their various undergraduate liberal-arts fields. The result of these discussions would be the designing and offering of a selection of courses in the content areas, team taught by liberal-arts and education faculty. For example, general courses in writing, literature, mathematics, geography, political science, or physics would be taught, making use of concrete lab experiences, inquiry methods, pair problem-solving techniques, heuristics, or any other alternative pedagogy that the team decides upon. Not only would the liberal-arts content be the focus, but time would be given for reflection and discussion in relation to the pedagogy used, as described in Chapters 3, 4, and 5. In this way, students themselves would become part of the community of discourse, and faculty and students alike would benefit from the processing of the instructional methods.

Team-taught courses, designed by the community and taught from its perspective, not only stand a better chance of being meaningful to the undergraduates in terms of the liberal-arts content, but they may serve as a powerful influence in overriding pedagogical schemes based on being the recipient, for years, of traditional teaching. According to Goodlad (1987), the offering of alternative models is one of the most needed changes in teacher education. After reviewing the data from observations in 1,016 classrooms, he concluded that

> the range of pedagogical methods observed is exceedingly narrow and these reflect methods observed by prospective teachers during their years of being students. It appears that what happens to teachers in university programs is simply not deep and profound enough to tran-scend what they had observed teaching to be during those years be-fore. Further, what was modeled before is demonstrated again during student teaching and expected of them as teachers. Were we to set out to design a system carefully contrived to preserve the status quo and perpetuate the conventional wisdom, it would be difficult to design one better. [p. 9]

Team-taught courses would be open to all undergraduates and would carry with them the possibility of earning joint credits in liberal arts and pre-education. This recommendation is in line with the Association of American Colleges' 1985 report, which stated that colleges will not improve the curriculum if they only emphasize content without getting to the heart of the matter: quality of teaching. The report even specifically calls for "active learning" and for faculty members to join together in "think tanks" and to open their classrooms to each other. Miami-Dade Community College has already established a Teaching–Learning Project, which offers a course to help university instructors become "classroom researchers" able to study how their students learn effectively and to teach accordingly (Heller, 1987).

The Graduate Program

Upon completing the pre-education baccalaureate, prospective teachers apply for entrance to the graduate program.

Graduate seminars would engage students in investigatory field work (described in Chapters 2, 3, 4, and 5) on various topics such as general cognition, science and math concepts, language arts, integrated arts, or social studies concepts. In place of traditional methods courses, these seminars would involve prospective teachers in immediately exploring what children know about certain topics and how this knowledge changes with development and experience. Different techniques of teaching the concepts would also be investigated. Video technology might be used to record investigatory sessions, so that diagnoses of children's understanding could be discussed and reflections on the teaching shared. In this way, prospective teachers would be engaged in critical and creative thinking about pedagogy. Rather then being *told* what developmental psychologists have found, they would become psychologists themselves. Rather than being *told* how to teach, they would construct their own pedagogy. This is not to say that all educational research should be disregarded. Instead, it would be shared in the seminars, when appropriate, in relation to prospective teachers' questions and needs in their investigations. This makes the research meaningful and pertinent to classroom practice, rather than simply being more information that must be committed to memory until the need for it to be applied occurs.

After completion of the investigatory fieldwork, a cooperative field experience would begin in the public school attached to the graduate center (described in Chapter 2 as a "portal system"). A seminar, dealing with issues that arise during the experience and team taught by teachers of the "portal system" and graduate center faculty, would accompany the fieldwork. (The reader should recall here that it was recommended in Chapter 2 that graduate center faculty be encouraged to take sabbatical semesters to teach as classroom teachers, as well, in the portal systems.) In this way, new instructional ideas and pedagogical research will have direct connection to the public schools. Ideas will grow out of classroom practice and affect classroom practice by the fact that the graduate centers are directly linked to the public schools. In the words of Goodlad (1987),

> For schools to get better, they must have better teachers, special educators, and administrators; universities must have access to school settings exhibiting the very best practices. To assure the best practices, schools must have ongoing access to alternative ideas and knowledge. For universities to have access to exemplary settings and for these settings to become and remain exemplary, the schools and the preparing institutions must enjoy a symbiotic relationship — of joining as equal partners. [pp. 9–10]

Following a semester of cooperative fieldwork, students (with the help of an advisor) would choose a question to research during their reflective fieldwork experience. As pointed out in Chapter 2, research questions may take many varying forms, such as a study of how children's writing changes between kindergarten and third grade, an analysis of the value of play to learning, a study of the development of an understanding of fractions, or a focused study on an alternative model of teaching and its results. Seminars dealing with various alternative philosophies and models of teaching, or educational structure and change, might be taken concurrently with the reflective fieldwork experience. The purpose of these seminars would be to enlarge students' frames of reference and to expand the critical discourse on institutions, their connections to society, and pathways to facilitating change within them.

Integrative fieldwork, or the clinical fellowship year, as introduced in Chapter 2, would complete the master's program. During this phase, the student would be employed as a novice teacher in a public school (not the one affiliated with the graduate center) and receive a "resource" faculty member from the graduate center as consultant/mentor. The mentor would visit approximately once a week and aid and support the novice, in order to insure a smooth transition and the application of what was learned during professional preparation to full-time classroom practice. A seminar would also be offered during this period to facilitate group brainstorming and sharing, as well as to provide an opportunity for mentoring, as described in Chapter 6.

After a successful CFY year, and with the master's degree completed, certification would be granted by the graduate center. With certification in hand, the teacher would then apply to the state for a license to practice.

Advanced Graduate Work

Although permanent certification would be achieved at the completion of the master's degree, advanced graduate work needs to be available, as well as encouraged. As "empowered" professionals, teachers deserve the right to apply for paid, sabbatical leaves every six years or so (in a similar fashion to professors), in order to engage in research at graduate centers. Duckworth (1987a) describes teaching and research as inseparable, since "good" teachers consider first how to engage learners with phenomena to create inquiry, then research learners' understanding in order to readjust the phenomena. In this way, curriculum evolves from the teacher/learner interaction. As she points out, however, teachers need time away from direct responsibilities of teaching, in order to focus their inquiry, reflect, and disseminate their ideas.

Deirdre, a junior high science teacher and a graduate student of mine, serves as an example. Deirdre's school was beginning a three-year project of curriculum revision in science when Deirdre applied for a sabbatical. She was interested in curriculum and spent the year studying various curriculum models and their philosophies, foundations, and implementation. She specifically focused on science and also investigated her students' understanding of two separate concepts: tidal change and density. Returning to her school the following fall, she became the chair of the curriculum revision project, and I joined her as consultant. Over the course of the next two years, the curriculum committee designed a hands-on, project-oriented science curriculum for the district. Deirdre and I also teamed up to lead a workshop for teachers the following year, at the annual conference of the Association for Constructivist Teaching. Deirdre illustrates an "empowered" teacher involved in advanced graduate work, but her case also illustrates how a school district can benefit from granting sabbaticals. She returned to her district with renewed enthusiasm, new ideas, and a commitment to change.

This book, itself, is illustrative of the type of research advanced graduate students might do. It began with an inquiry into teacher education, described and analyzed the process of teaching I've been engaged in during the last several years in answer to my inquiry, and by so doing described a program of pedagogy for teacher educators. It involved inquiry and reflection and culminated in a proposal for action. If teachers were given the opportunity periodically to reflect on a question of their own interest, a body of research would develop, regarding classroom teaching and learning, that might be both beneficial to other teachers and promote further investigations.

DIFFERENTIATED TEACHING LEVELS AND PAY SCALES

Although differentiated teaching levels and corresponding pay scales have been recommended already by various reports (Carnegie Forum, 1986; Holmes Group, 1986), the process of selecting teachers on the basis of merit has been a debatable issue. With the establishment of graduate centers and incentives for advanced graduate work, teachers would have to apply for the staff positions in these institutions. A desire for experimentation and innovation would be a primary factor in both hiring at the center and in the granting of sabbaticals. Because the work demands of teachers involved in the centers would be greater than that of regular classroom teachers, a pay increase should come with these positions, as well as for the successful completion of advanced graduate work. In this way, teachers are given goals they can strive for in a system that rewards both innovative experimentation and research. Three levels of professional status naturally result: clinical fellows, licensed teachers, and graduate center teachers (or those completing a certain amount of advanced graduate work at the center).

CONCLUSION

A model of the teacher as researcher has been delineated in this book as a proposal for teacher education. The model involves the establishment of graduate centers of education with linkages to the university and the public schools. Based on the philosophies of phronesis and constructivism, the model has called for the establishment of communities of discourse engaged in reflection, conversation, and action. Research has been defined as investigations regarding children's understanding as well as inquiry into the structures of subject matter. Courses have been suggested that (1) engage teachers as learners and then focus reflection on the pedagogy and learning involved, (2) develop an understanding of the connections between disciplines and the modes of inquiry involved in them, and (3) investigate how learners "know" and "come to know." Various field experiences have been described and illustrated, from beginning investigatory experiences to the culminating integrative experience with mentoring.

The book began with an inquiry about teacher education and a reflection about Jessica and her learning. It has presented chapters of discourse, both mine and other teachers. It ends with a call to action. To meet the demands of the new teaching role presented here, teachers need to be educated not as technicians, but as professionals; not as skilled imitators, but as problem posers and solvers. True reform in education will not succeed until teachers are able to act as articulate, empowered agents of change.

Appendix

Course Descriptions for the Interdisciplinary Thought Major

Further information is presented here on the courses described in Chapter 7 that form the core of the interdisciplinary major proposed at Southern Connecticut State University. The course descriptions are adapted here with permission from SCSU. Readers are reminded that the three strands of the major are (1) arts and humanities, (2) social sciences, and (3) natural sciences.

SOPHOMORE COURSE: INTRODUCTION TO INTERDISCIPLINARY THOUGHT

The introductory course in Interdisciplinary Thought is required of all students in this major, regardless of which strand they may later choose. Although the aims, method, and basic structure of this course will remain constant, each time it is taught a different topic may be selected. Whatever the topic, it will be general enough to be examined from the points of view of all three faculty participants representing each strand in the major. New reading and writing assignments, lectures, and subjects for discussion will be planned accordingly. This method will encourage the faculty to rethink the course regularly, thereby enhancing its value to the students. The course is divided into three parts, with each professor presenting a separate section, but with all using the following skeletal outline, regardless of the topic selected.

1. Definitions of the topic within the strand; short paper defining the topic due second period
2. Application of definitions of topic to a specific example in the strand
3. Application of definition of topic to other examples drawn from other disciplines in the strand; exploration of connections and differences in thought

4. Investigation of alternative methodologies to define topic
5. Critique of methodology used in definition

Sample Topic.   One possible topic for the course is revolution. The concept of revolution is derived from the natural science field of celestial mechanics, but has its root contemporary meaning in the arena of social organization and upheaval. At the same time, natural scientists and humanists have characterized dramatic shifts of theory, practice, or consciousness as "revolutions" in their spheres of study. The following questions serve as possible discussion points as students attempt to define revolution within each strand (objective #1 in the skeletal outline).

1. What sorts of change qualify as "revolutionary"? Does it depend on the amount of change, the speed of change, the particular things that change, or what?
2. Whose perceptions establish that a revolution has occurred or is under way?
3. Do revolutions always arise out of, or give rise to, conflict with earlier systems of order, thought, or consciousness?
4. Do revolutions always go "forward," or can they also go "backward"?
5. How fundamental are the changes wrought by a revolution? Is human nature, or the nature of human understanding or experience, ever transformed into something totally "new" and disconnected from the past, or are such claims illusory?
6. Why do some people embrace revolutionary changes while others resist or reject them?
7. Are revolutions in human practice and experience matters of human voluntary choice, or are they inevitable?
8. Is revolution different from evolution?
9. What are the principal nonrevolutionary modes of change in practice or experience?

Arts and Humanities Section

A. *Specific example to study:* The case of Michelangelo Merisi da Caravaggio (1573–1609). Premise: Caravaggio has been considered the preeminent revolutionary artist by critics and historians (Baglione, Bellori, Berenson, Hibbard), but his reputation as a revolutionary must be reevaluated in light of new evidence.
   1. Biography: Caravaggio's "revolutionary" personality, police records concerning unconventional behavior, lawsuit brought against him by a conventional painter

2. Analysis of selected works (*Bacchus*, Florence, Uffizi; *Supper at Emmaus*, London, National Gallery; *St. Matthew Writing His Gospel*, destroyed)

    a. Why these works have been considered revolutionary
   - (1) Stylistic anomalies shown by comparing with works of art by Caravaggio's predecessors and contemporaries
   - (2) Demonstration of lasting impact of these works—how they changed the history of art

    b. Aspects of the paintings that are nonrevolutionary
   - (1) Style dependent upon conventional art of Northern Italy
   - (2) Themes and interpretations echo those of the official Catholic Counter-Reformation

    c. Conclusions
   - (1) Only certain aspects of Caravaggio's art may be called revolutionary
   - (2) We can only assess the revolutionary in art by understanding the historical context

    d. Discussion regarding the nature of revolutionary art (technical/theoretical, ethical, aesthetic)

3. *Reading:* On Caravaggio the revolutionary and Caravaggio the product of counterrevolution

B. Analysis of the definition and assumptions used in (A)
1. Stylistic analysis
2. Iconography
(What are these methods? What are their strengths and weaknesses? How do they relate to methods in the social and natural sciences?)

C. Application of definition and methodology to examples from other disciplines within the arts and humanities. Specific examples chosen will be decided by students and instructor. (Suggestions: Mozart, Henry James, Chomsky, Socrates, James Joyce, Debussy, Cézanne, Locke, Picasso)

Social Sciences Section

A. *Specific example to study:* The U.S. Revolution of 1776 and the Nicaraguan Revolution of 1979. Premise: The U.S. Revolution is commonly accepted as a "revolution." In what sense is that term used? Is it appropriate? Does it apply as well to the Nicaraguan Revolution of 1979?

1. Two different analytical models will be used: The "Western liberal" interpretation and the Marxist materialist model.
2. Discussion will have the following foci:
   a. Revolutions as history: Do all revolutions have common stages?
   b. Social structure: Pre- and postrevolution
   c. Economics: Pre- and postrevolution
   d. Politics: Pre- and postrevolution
      (1) Patterns of regulation
      (2) Patterns of justification
   e. Geography: Pre- and postrevolution
   f. Consciousness and revolution: When did new perceptions and values crystallize?
   g. Which modes of experience were affected: technical/theoretical, ethical, aesthetic?

B. Analysis of the definition and assumptions used in (A)
1. Western liberal perspective
2. Marxist/materialist perspective
   (What are these methods? What are their strengths and weaknesses? What are their biases?)

C. How do political revolutions compare and contrast with revolutions in social practice and/or in thought about society? Specific examples chosen will be decided by students and instructor. (Suggestions: Industrial Revolution, Watson and the rise of behaviorism, Keynesian revolution in economics, Durkheim's structural revolution, Werner's or Piaget's interactionism, French Revolution of 1789, Cuban Revolution of 1959, Nicaraguan Revolution)

Natural Sciences Section

A. *Specific example to study:* The case of Antoine Laurent Lavoisier, discoverer of oxygen
1. Biography: Lavoisier's revolutionary personality. Attempted to introduce reforms in the French monetary and taxation system and in farming methods. Arrested and tried by the French Revolutionary Tribunal; guillotined May 8, 1794.
2. Analysis of his conception and discovery of oxygen
   a. Revolution in concept of chemical change
   b. Revolution in concept of matter
   c. Revolution in form of chemical experimentation: rise of quantitative experimentation

3. Effect on technical/theoretical, ethical, and aesthetic modes of experience in chemistry

B. Analysis of the definition and assumptions used in (A)
1. Kuhn's view of normal revolution: revolution as evolution
2. Popper's view of revolution: revolution as contradiction
3. Bloor's view of revolution: the societal context

C. Application of definition and methodology to examples from other disciplines within the natural sciences. Specific examples chosen will be decided by students and instructor. (Suggestions: Pythagoras, Bacon and inductive reasoning, Descartes (Cartesian logic and deductive reasoning), the Newtonian revolution, Darwinian revolution, Faraday and Maxwell, Einstein and relativity theory, Bohr and quantum mechanics, continental drift and plate tectonics)

Bibliography

Arendt, H. *On Revolution*. New York: Penguin Books, 1977.

Armitage, A. *Copernicus: The Founder of Modern Astronomy*. New York, London: Thomas Yoseloff, 1957.

Bellone, E. *A World on Paper: Studies on the Second Scientific Revolution*. Trans. Mirella and Piccardo Giacconi. Cambridge, MA; London: MIT Press, 1980.

Bellone, E. "The Structure of the Atom." Nobel Lecture, Dec. 11, 1922. In *Nobel Lectures, Physics, 1922-1941* (pp. 7–43). Amsterdam, New York: Published for the Nobel Foundation by Elsevier, 1964.

Bloor, D. *Knowledge and Social Imagery*. London: Routledge and Kegan Paul, 1976.

Bowler, P. J. *The Eclipse of Darwinism: Anti-Darwinian Evolution Theories in the Decades Around 1900*. Baltimore, MD; London: Johns Hopkins University Press, 1983.

Brinton, C. *Anatomy of Revolution*. New York: Vintage Books, 1965.

Cedarbaum, D. G. "Paradigms." *Study in History and Philosophy of Science*, *14*, 173–213, 1983.

Cohen, I. B. *Revolution in Science*. Cambridge, MA; London: Belknap Press, 1985.

Croce, B. *Aesthetic*. New York, 1909.

Davies, J. C. "Towards a Theory of Revolution." *American Sociological Review*, *27*, (1) 5–19, 1962.

Douglas, E. P. *Rebels and Democrats*. Chicago: Quadrangle Books, 1965.

Einstein, A., & Infeld, L. *The Evolution of Physics: The Growth of Ideas from Early Concepts to Relativity and Quanta*. New York: Simon & Schuster, 1938.

Friedlaender, W. *Caravaggio Studies*. New York: Schocken Books, 1984.

Gough, J. B. "Some Early References to Revolutions in Chemistry." *Ambix, 29,* 106–109, 1982.

Gutting, G., (Ed.). *Paradigms and Revolutions: Applications and Appraisals of Thomas Kuhn's Philosophy of Science.* Notre Dame, IN: University of Notre Dame Press, 1980.

Hacking, I., (Ed.). *Scientific Revolutions.* Oxford, London, New York: Oxford University Press, 1981.

Hanson, N. R. "Copernicus' Role in Kant's Revolution." *Journal of the History of Ideas, 20,* 274–281, 1959.

Hanson, N. R. "The Copernican Disturbance and the Keplerian Revolution." *Journal of the History of Ideas, 22,* 169–184, 1961.

Hauser, A. *Philosophy of Art History.* New York: Knauf, 1958.

Hibbard, H. *Caravaggio.* New York: Harper & Row, 1983.

Himmelfarb, G. *Darwin and the Darwinian Revolution.* Garden City, NY: Doubleday, 1959.

Hull, D. L. *Darwin and His Critics: The Reception of Darwin's Theory of Evolution by the Scientific Community.* Cambridge, MA: Harvard University Press, 1973.

Kleinbauer, W. *Modern Perspectives in Western Art History.* New York: Holt, Rinehart & Winston, 1971.

Kuhn, T. S. *The Structure of Scientific Revolutions,* 2nd rev. ed. Chicago: University of Chicago Press, 1970.

Kuhn, T. S. *The Essential Tension: Selected Studies in Scientific Tradition and Change.* Chicago, London: University of Chicago Press, 1977.

Main, J. T. *The Social Structure of Revolutionary America.* Princeton, NJ: Princeton University Press, 1965.

Martin, J. K. *Men in Rebellion.* New Brunswick, NJ: Rutgers University Press, 1973.

Mayr, E. "Cause and Effect in Biology." *Science, 134,* 1501–1506, 1961.

Mayr, E. *The Growth of Biological Thought: Diversity, Evolution, and Inheritance.* Cambridge, MA; London: Belknap Press, 1982.

Pais, A. *"Subtle is the Lord . . . ": The Science and the Life of Albert Einstein.* New York: Oxford University Press, 1982.

Panofsky, E. "The History of Art As a Humanistic Discipline." In E. Panofsky (Ed.) *Meaning in the Visual Arts.* New York: Doubleday, 1955.

Roskill, M. *What Is Art History?* New York: Harper & Row, 1976.

Vilas, C. M. *The Sandinista Revolution: National Liberation and Social Transformation in Central America.* New York: Monthly Review Press, 1986.

JUNIOR-YEAR PERSPECTIVES COURSES

Perspectives in the Arts and Humanities

This course will not be the same every time it is taught; the specific content (objects of study, methodologies) will undoubtedly change with the instructors' expertise. It will, however, always compare and contrast various methodologies in at least two disciplines in the arts and humanities. For this sample outline, the following works are to be the objects of the analyses:

Art
  Leonardo da Vinci, *Madonna and St Anne*, London, N.G.
  Michelangelo, *Moses*, Rome, S. Pietro in Vincoli
  Claude Monet, *Haystacks*, London, Tate Gallery
  Piano and Rogers, *Pompidou Centre*, Paris

Literature
  Sophocles, *Oedipus Rex*
  Shakespeare, sonnets
  Joseph Conrad, *Heart of Darkness*
  Thomas Pynchon, "Entropy"

The following is a syllabus focusing on art and literature:

A. Personal impressions
   1. *Reading*
      Walter Pater, *The Renaissance: Studies in Art and Poetry, 1894*. New York: Macmillan, Ch. 1: "Leonardo da Vinci."
      Matthew Arnold, *Essays in Criticism*, S. R. Littlewood, ed. London: Macmillan, 1960.
   2. Writing: Personal impression of either Leonardo or Conrad
B. Formalism
   1. *Reading*
      Heinrich Wolfflin, *Classic Art*. New York: Phaedon, 1953. Ch. 2: "Leonardo da Vinci."
      Cleanth Brooks and Robert Heilman, *Understanding Drama*. New York: Holt, 1948.
   2. Writing: Formal analysis of either Leonardo or Conrad
C. Iconography/thematic studies
   1. *Reading*
      Erwin Panofsky, "Iconography and Iconology." In E. Panofsky (Ed.) *Meaning in the Visual Arts*. New York: Doubleday, 1955.

Cleanth Brooks (Ed.), *Tragic Themes in Western Literature.*
New Haven, CT: Yale University Press, 1955.

2.   Thematic or iconographic analysis of Leonardo or Conrad

D. Archetypal analysis

1. *Reading*

Carl Jung, *The Symbolic Life.* Princeton, NJ: Princeton University Press, 1976.

2.   Writing: Archetypal analysis of either Leonardo or Conrad

E. Freudian analysis

1. *Reading*

Sigmund Freud, *Leonardo da Vinci and a Memory of his Childhood.* New York: Norton, 1964.

Patrick Mullahy, *Oepidus: Myth and Complex.* New York: Hermitage, 1948.

2.   Writing: Freudian analysis of either Leonardo or Conrad

F. Marxist analysis

1. *Reading*

Selections from T. J. Clark, *Images of the People: Gustave Courbet and the 1848 Revolution.* Greenwich, CT: New York Graphic Society, 1973.

Frederick Jameson, *Art's Enigma.* New York: John Lane, 1911.

2.   Writing: Marxist analysis of Leonardo or Conrad

G. Structuralism

1. *Reading*

Claude Lévi-Strauss, *Myth and Meaning.* New York, Schocken Books, 1979.

2.   Writing: Structural analysis of Leonardo or Conrad

H. Deconstruction

1. *Reading*

Jonathan Culler, *The Pursuit of Signs: Semiotics, Literature, Deconstruction.* Ithaca, NY: Cornell University Press, 1981.

2.   Writing: Deconstruction of Leonardo or Conrad

I. Feminism

1. *Reading*

Selections from Norma Broude and Mary Garrard (Ed.), *Feminism and Art History: Questioning the Litany.* New York: Harper and Row, 1982.

Selections from Sandra Gilbert and Susan Gubar (Ed.), *Shakespeare's Sisters: Feminist Essays on Women Poets.* Bloomington: Indiana University Press, 1979.

2.   Writing: Feminist analysis of Leonardo or Conrad

Perspectives and Interpretations in the Social Sciences

To exemplify the features of social science, this course focuses on a theme or problem that is found universally in human cultural systems and has been an object of study from several disciplinary perspectives. Examples of such themes include childhood, education, deviance, communication, status, health and illness, family, religion, technology, and work and play. Regardless of the theme, which will be chosen by the faculty team each time the course is offered, the following format will be used.

1. Presentation, through readings and class discussions, of a number of brief examples of the theme, in different cultural settings, reflecting different issues about the theme that have engaged social scientists. Discussion of this material as a means of introducing subsequent units of the course and the questions they explore.
2. Identification of a particular practical or theoretical problem regarding the theme which has been raised in some cultural system and/or social science discipline. Focus on how the problem arose for investigators.
3. Examination of research findings from at least two social science disciplines bearing on this problem and/or examination of findings from at least two different cultures with contrasting patterns for handling the thematic issue.
4. Reflection on modes of social inquiry: How did the social investigators define their research problem? Did their methods bias their conclusions in an unreasonable (i.e., question-begging) way? How much confidence can we have in their data? To what extent can their conclusions be generalized?
5. Repetition of steps 2 through 4 for each additional unit in the course.
6. Brief writing assignments for some of the units, plus a semester project (term paper or journal), plus an essay examination as means of evaluation.

Following is a course outline for the theme of work and play.

A.   Introduction: What makes work, work; and play, play?
    I.   Goals
        a.   To discover the diversity of forms and functions of play and work as these are exemplified in different times and cultures
        b.   To foreshadow topics taken up in later units of the course
        c.   To have students begin reflection on their own work and play activity in the light of others' experiences

2. Class and homework activity: Discussion of materials; completion of a questionnaire on student's own experience and attitudes toward work and play; completion of short personal essay entitled, "The Development of My Attitudes About Work
and Play"

B. Historical accounts: If work and play are not always and every-
where the same, why and how have they changed?

    1. Goals

        a. To offer a first effort at systematizing the evidence of di-
versity in patterns of work and play

        b. To consider how history as a form of inquiry interprets
facts in order to "explain" them

    2. *Readings*

        a. B. Sutton-Smith, "The Spirit of Play." In G. Fein and M.
Rivkin (Eds.), *The Young Child at Play: Reviews of Re-
search*, (Vol. 1, pp. 3–15). Washington, D.C.: National
Association for the Education of Young Children, 1986.

        b. Excerpts from H. Arendt, *The Human Condition.* Chica-
go, Ill.: University of Chicago Press, 1958.

        c. Excerpts from F. Braudel, *The Structures of Everyday
Life: Civilization and Capitalism, 15th–18th Century*
(Vol. 1). New York: Harper and Row, 1982.

C. Functional accounts: Do work and play have particular functions
to perform in sustaining a social system?

    Readings

        a. R. Saltz and E. Saltz, "Pretend Play Training and Its Out-
comes." In G. Fein and M. Rivkin (Eds.) *op. cit.*, pp.
155–174.

        b. Excerpts from G. W. Domhoff, *The Bohemian Grove and
Other Retreats: A Study in Ruling-class Cohesiveness.*
New York: Harper and Row, 1974.

        c. Excerpts from E. Durkheim, *The Division of Labor in
Society.* New York: Free Press of Glencoe, 1964.

D. Structural accounts: How does analysis of forms structures and
patterns of interaction explain phenomena of work and play?

    Readings

        a. Excerpts from J. Piaget, *Play, Dreams and Imitation in
Childhood.* New York: Norton, 1962.

        b. L. McCune, "Symbolic Development in Normal and
Atypical Infants." In G. Fein and M. Rivkin (Eds.) *op.
cit.*, pp. 45–62.

        c. Excerpts from G. Friedmann, *Anatomy of Work: Labor,*

Leisure and the Implication of Automation. New York: Free Press of Glencoe, 1961.

    d.   E. Mandel, *Marxist Economic Theory* (Vol. 1). New York: Monthly Review Press, 1969.

E. Developmental accounts: Are there regularities of evolution or growth which control the qualities of play or work in our lives?

    Readings

    a.   Excerpts from E. Erikson, *Toys and Reasons.* New York: Norton, 1977.

    b.   C. Muller-Schwarze (Ed.), *Evolution of Play Behavior.* Stroudsburg, Pa.: Dowden, Hutchinson and Ross, 1977.

    c.   Excerpts from H. Braverman, *Labor and Monopoly Capital: The Degradation of Work in the Twentieth Century.* New York: Monthly Review Press, 1975.

    d.   D. Gordon, R. Edwards, and M. Reich, *Segmented Work, Divided Workers.* New York: Cambridge University Press, 1982.

F. Motivation: What makes people work or play: The role of internal needs and drives and of external stimuli

    Readings

    a.   Excerpts from D. Berlyne, *Conflict, Arousal, and Curiosity.* New York: McGraw-Hill, 1960.

    b.   Excerpts from I. Breatherton (Ed.), *Symbolic Play: The Development of Social Understanding.* Orlando, Fla.: Academic Press, 1984.

    c.   R. M. Kanter and B. Stein (Eds.), *Life in Organizations: Workplaces as People Experience Them.* New York: Basic Books, 1979.

    d.   Excerpts from R. M. Kanter, *The Change Masters: Innovation for Productivity in the American Corporation.* New York: Simon and Schuster, 1983.

G. Gender: How and why do men and women differ in their patterns of work and play?

    Readings

    a.   Excerpts from P. Voydanoff (Ed.), *Work and Family Life.* Newbury Park, Calif.: Sage Pub., 1987.

    b.   Excerpts from J. A. Matthaei, *An Economic History of Women in America.* New York: Schocken, 1982.

    c.   M. Liss (Ed.), *Social and Cognitive Skills: Sex Roles and Children's Play.* New York: Academic Press, 1983.

H. Work, play, and fulfillment: Under what circumstances is work or play gratifying for the participant?

Readings
a. Excerpts from J. Huizinga, *Homo Ludens*. Boston: Beacon Press, 1950.
b. Excerpts from J. Vanek, (Ed.), *Self-Management*. Baltimore: Penguin, 1975.
c. Excerpts from E. Fromm, *The Sane Society*. New York: Fawcett, 1985.
d. Excerpts from Aristotle, *Politics*. New York: Cambridge University Press, 1988.
e. Excerpts from M. Csikszentmhalyi, *Beyond Boredom and Anxiety*. San Francisco: Jossey-Bass, 1975.

I. Work, play, and deprivation: Under what circumstances is work or play burdensome for the participant?
Readings
a. Excerpts from R. Blauner, *Alienation and Freedom: The Factory Worker and His Industry*. Chicago: Chicago University Press, 1964.
b. Excerpts from E. Fromm, *The Sane Society*. New York: Fawcett, 1985.
c. Excerpts from E. Mandel, *Marxist Economic Theory* (Vol. 2). New York: Monthly Review Press, 1969.

J. Explanation and social science: How do social scientists "explain" things, and what, if anything, makes it "scientific"?
Readings
a. Excerpts from A. MacIntyre, *After Virtue*. Notre Dame, Indiana: University of Notre Dame Press, 1984.
b. D. Braybrooke, *Philosophical Problems of the Social Sciences*. New York: Macmillan, 1965.

Perspectives on the Nature of Thinking in the Natural Sciences

The flexible design of this course will permit faculty from any of the natural science disciplines to teach the course on an individual or team basis. Each section of the course will involve the students reading articles, excerpts from books, and monographs that illustrate the points under discussion. Students will be expected to participate in active classroom discussions, abstract and comment upon the readings, and submit a series of short papers throughout the semester. The following course syllabus is a model that will be followed by faculty members teaching the course. Modifications in case studies and readings will be made to accommodate the course needs, on an annual basis.

1. *Science vs. nonscience.* This section of the course will compare and contrast scientific thinking with nonscientific thinking strategies. The topics to be discussed may include, but will not necessarily be limited to, the following:
   Creationism vs. the theory of evolution
   Unidentified flying objects vs. identified flying objects
   Astrology vs. predictive behavior
2. *The scientific method.* The scientific method will be defined and applied to a current topic of scientific investigation. Potential areas of investigation in this section of the course include the following:
   Acid precipitation: Experimental design and evaluation
   Nuclear night: Experimental evidence and extrapolation
   Food and famine: Agricultural research strategies
   AIDS: Medical models and the scientific method
   Superconductors: Old methodology for new research areas
3. *Research strategies within the sciences.* A variety of strategies for investigating scientific questions will be explored. The major areas for investigation will be drawn from the following:
   Qualitative vs. quantitative analysis
   Field vs. laboratory studies
   Observation vs. experimentation
4. *Science vs. nonscience revisited.* The course will end with a discussion of student papers that focus on the nature of scientific thought and its application to the solution of a specific question. The scientific method will be utilized to demythologize some popular ideas about "science" and pseudoscience.

The bibliography for this course will by necessity be developed by the instructor of record for any given semester. However, it should be noted that the general reading list will include several articles of recent origin which deal with the topics for discussion and debate. In addition, it is recommended that the following references be included as beginning points for reading in this course:

Cole, S., Cole, J. R., & Simon, G. A. "Chance and Consensus in Peer Review." *Science, 214,* 881–886, 1981.
Lederman, L. M. "The Value of Fundamental Science." *Scientific American, 251*(5), 47, 1984.
Medawar, P. B. *Advice to a Young Scientist.* New York: Harper & Row, 1979.

SENIOR-YEAR SEMINARS

The third course in the core sequence of the Interdisciplinary Thought major is to be a high-level senior seminar dealing with problem posing and solving, resources, and research within the chosen strand. Its goal is to have students put into intensive practice some of the interdisci-plinary precepts learned in the first two core courses, taken in the sophomore and junior years.

The course format for these senior seminars, regardless of the chosen strand, is as follows:

1. *Problem Definition and Research Procedures*. The course will begin with sessions on problem definition. What is a topic? What do you want to find out? How can you narrow your field of inquiry? Students will be assisted in selecting topics for systematic analysis. Project proposals will be drawn up by students. Research procedures appropriate for acquiring information on selected topics will be discussed.
2. *Seminar Speaker Series*. Experts dealing with areas closely related to problems defined by the students will be invited to present their views in class. This segment of the course will provide an opportunity for identifying and analyzing various issues of concern. Special attention will be given to problem posing and solving. The interchange among students, faculty, and the outside experts will permit an evaluation of different methods and theories.
3. *Student Seminar Presentations*. Students will present their research findings to their peers, instructors, and invited guests. Each presentation will be followed by a question-and-answer session. A report of the findings will be placed on file in the office of the Interdisciplinary Studies coordinator.

Seminar in the Arts and Humanities

This course focuses on a broad subject in the arts and humanities, chosen by the instructor in consultation with the students in the seminar. Examples of sample course topics include self-reference, the comic, the tragic, the satiric, the classic, the romantic, and modernism. The subject chosen will serve as the focus for independent research by class members. Students will learn how to develop a thesis topic by posing a problem in this subject, which draws on at least two disciplines within the humanities. Each student will be expected to pursue intensive study of this specific problem by using the multiple perspectives of the interdisciplinary approach. In addition to periodic presentations, a final thesis will be required of each student.

This seminar is not solely an independent study course, for the plan is to increase individual students' understanding of interdisciplinary study, not only through their own work, but also through the diverse perspectives that others bring to a similar problem. Once again, we want students to learn that what we desire to know helps to determine what we do know. Though the course culminates in a research paper, we envision that the students will understand that the amount of information in the humanities is limited only by the questions they pose and that their learning can continue beyond the course.

Seminar in the Social Sciences

This course will function as a capstone course in the social sciences strand of the Interdisciplinary Thought major. It will provide students with an opportunity for the systematic analysis of a problem in the social sciences that is of special interest to them. Topics for investigation will be selected by the student, with the approval of the instructor. Special attention will be given to problem posing and solving and to critical research, as indicated by the course format presented earlier.

Seminar in the Natural Sciences

This course will function as a capstone course in the natural sciences strand of the Interdisciplinary Thought major. It will provide students with an opportunity for the systematic analysis of a natural science problem that is of special interest to them. Topics for investigation will be selected by the student, with the approval of the instructor. Special attention will be given to problem posing and solving and to critical scientific research, as indicated by the course format presented earlier.

References

A nation at risk: The report of the National Commission on Excellence in Education. (1983). Washington, DC: NCEE.

Armstrong, M. (1980). *Closely observed children: The diary of a primary classroom.* London: Writers and Readers.

Bandura, A., & Walters, R. H. (1963). *Social learning and personality development.* New York: Holt, Rinehart and Winston.

Barzun, J. (1968). *The American university: How it runs, where it is going.* New York: Harper & Row.

Berliner, D. (1986). In pursuit of the expert pedagogue. *Educational Researcher, 15*(7), 5–13.

Beyer, L. E. (1986). Beyond elitism and technicism: Teacher education as practical philosophy. *Journal of Teacher Education, 37*(2), 37–41.

Bissex, G. (1980). *GYNS at WRK: A child learns to write and read.* Cambridge, MA: Harvard University Press.

Bloom, B. (1976). *Human characteristics and school learning.* New York: McGraw-Hill.

Brandt, R. (1986). On the expert teacher: A conversation with David Berliner. *Educational Leadership, 44*(2), 4–9.

Calkins, L. (1986). *The art of teaching writing.* Portsmouth, NH: Heinemann Press.

Carnegie Forum on Education and the Economy. (1986). *A nation prepared: Teachers for the 21st century.* Hyattsville, MD: Carnegie Forum.

Chomsky, N. (1957). *Syntactic structures.* The Hague: Mouton.

Clark, C., & Lampert, M. (1986, September/October). The study of teacher thinking: Implications for teacher education. *Journal of Teacher Education, 37*(5) 27–31.

Cleveland, H. (1986). Educating citizens and leaders for an information-based society. *Educational Leadership, 44,* 62–64.

Comfort, A. (1984). *Reality and empathy: Physics, mind, and science in the 21st century.* New York: Paragon House.

Connecticut General Assembly. (1986, May). Educational Enhancement Act, Bill #1001.

DeBono, E. (1986, January/February). Beyond critical thinking. *Curriculum Review,* 13–16.

DeVane, W. C. (1957). *The American university in the twentieth century.* Baton Rouge: Louisiana State University Press.

Doyle, W. (1977). Learning in the classroom environment: An ecological analysis. *Journal of Teacher Education, 28*(6), 51–55.

Duckworth, E. (1987a). *"The having of wonderful ideas" and other essays on teaching and learning.* New York: Teachers College Press.

Duckworth, E. (1987b, October 21–22). *Opening the world.* Keynote address, annual conference of the Association for Constructivist Teaching, West Point, New York.

Durkheim, E. (1954). *Elementary forms of the religious life.* New York: Free Press of Glencoe.

Fosnot, C. T. (1981). *Art as a problem solving activity.* Unpublished manuscript, University of Massachusetts, Amherst.

Fosnot, C. T. (1984). Media and technology in education: A constructivist view. *Educational Communication and Technology Journal, 32*(4), 195–205.

Fosnot, C. T. (1986). Curriculum: A dance of construction. *The Constructivist, 2*(1), 1–8.

Fosnot, C. T. (1988, January 13–19). *The dance of education.* Paper presented at the annual meeting of The Association for Educational Communication and Technology, New Orleans.

Fosnot, C. T., Forman, G., Edwards, C. P., & Goldhaber, J. (1988). The development of an understanding of balance and the effect of training via stop-action video. *Journal of Applied Developmental Psychology, 9*(1) 1–33.

Foster, G., & Pellens, S. (1986). Teacher development as metamorphosis. *Educational Science Forum, 11*, 1–10.

Friedman, M. I., Brinlee, P. S., & Hayes, P. B. (1980). *Improving teacher education: Resources and recommendations.* New York: Longman.

Gardner, H. (1985). *The mind's new science.* New York: Basic Books.

Geertz, C. (1980). Blurred genres. *American Scholar, 49*, Spring, 165–179.

Goldberg, M., & Harvey, J. (1983). A nation at risk: The report of the National Commission on Excellence in Education [Review]. *Phi Delta Kappan, 65*(1), 14–18.

Golomb, C. (1974). *Young children's sculpture and drawing.* Cambridge, MA: Harvard University Press.

Goodlad, J. (1983). *A place called school: Prospects for the future.* Reading, MA: McGraw-Hill.

Goodlad, J. (1987, Summer). School renewal and the education of educators: The partnership concept. *University of Massachusetts Newsletter*, pp. 9–11.

Graves, D. (1983). *Writing: Teachers and children at work.* Portsmouth, NH: Heinemann Press.

Graves, D. (1984). *A researcher learns to write.* Portsmouth, NH: Heinemann Press.

Gray, W. A., & Gray, M. M. (1985). Synthesis of research on mentoring beginning teachers. *Educational Leadership, 43*(3), 37–43.

Grennon, J. (1987). *Walking through the shadow: The journey of a first year teacher*. Doctoral dissertation, Columbia University, New York.

Haskins, C. H. (1923). *The rise of universities*. New York: Holt.

Hay, L. (1984, January 20–24). *A futurist's view of technology in education*. Invited address at the annual conference of the Association for Educational Communication and Technology, Dallas, Texas.

Heller, S. (1987, September 2). New wave of curricular reform: Connections between disciplines. *The Chronicle of Higher Education*, pp. A28–A34.

Henderson, E. H. (1981). *Teaching children to read and spell*. De Kalb: Northern Illinois University Press.

Henderson, E. H. (1985). *Teaching spelling*. Boston: Houghton-Mifflin.

Henderson, E. H., & Beers, J. W. (Eds.). (1980). *Developmental and cognitive aspects of learning to spell: A reflection of word knowledge*. Newark, DE: International Reading Association.

Holmes Group. (1986). *Tomorrow's teachers: A report of the Holmes Group*. East Lansing, MI: Holmes Group.

Howey, K. R. (1983). Teacher education: An overview. In K. R. Howey & W. E. Gardner (Eds.), *The education of teachers: A look ahead*. New York: Longman.

Inhelder, B., Sinclair, H., & Bovet, M. (1974). *Learning and the development of cognition*. Cambridge, MA: Harvard University Press.

Ives, W. S., & Meringoff, J. (1979). The role of artistic media in aesthetic development. In D. Perkins (Ed.), *Aesthetic development and arts education* (pp. 118–144). St. Louis: CEMREL.

Jackson, P. (1985, April 2). *The mimetic and the transformative: Legitimating visions of educational thought and practice*. Invited address at the annual meeting of AERA, Chicago.

Jones, E. (1975). Providing college-level role models for the socialization of elementary level open classroom teachers. *California Journal of Teacher Education*, 2(4), 33–51.

Joyce, B., & Showers, B. (1982). The coaching of teaching. *Educational Leadership, 40*(2), 4–10.

Kamii, C. (1985). *Young children reinvent arithmetic: Implications of Piaget's theory*. New York: Teachers College Press.

Kamii, C. (1989). Young children *continue to reinvent arithmetic — 2nd Grade: Implications of Piaget's theory*. New York: Teachers College Press.

Karmiloff-Smith, A., & Inhelder, B. (1974). If you want to get ahead, get a theory. *Cognition, 3*, 195–222.

Koetting, R. (1984). *Philosophical foundations and instructional design*. Paper presented at the annual meeting of The Association for Educational Communication and Technology, Dallas.

Koffka, K. (1935). *Principles of gestalt psychology*. New York: Harcourt Brace and World.

Kuhn, T. S. (1970). *The structure of scientific revolutions*. Chicago: University of Chicago Press.

Labinowicz, E. (1985). *Learning from children*. Menlo Park, CA: Addison-Wesley.

Leatherman, C. (1988, April 20). Reforms in education of school teachers face tough new challenges. *The Chronicle of Higher Education*, pp. A1–A31.

Lester, J. (1987). Math journals: An individualized program. *The Constructivist*, 2(2), 1–7.

Lévi-Strauss, C. (1963). *Structural anthropology*. New York: Basic Books.

Lochhead, J. (1977, June). *Teaching students how to learn*. Paper presented at the Third International Conference on Improving University Teaching, New Castle, Great Britain.

Murray, D. M. (1985). What happens when students learn to write. In J. Hansen, T. Newkirk, & D. Graves (Eds.), *Breaking ground: Teachers relate reading and writing in the elementary school*. Portsmouth, NH: Heinemann Press.

Murray, F. (1986). Goals for the reform of teacher education: An executive summary of the Holmes Group report. *Phi Delta Kappan*, 68(1), 28–32.

Neely, A. M. (1986). Planning and problem solving in teacher education. *Journal of Teacher Education*, 37(3) 29–33.

Nemser, S. F. (1983). Learning to teach. In L. S. Shulman & G. Sykes (Eds.), *Handbook of teaching and policy*, pp. 150–170. New York: Longman.

New Haven Register. (1985, September 15). Johnny can't read because he never gets a chance. p. E10.

Newport, J. F. (1983). Let's admit we can't train teachers — and ask for help. *Phi Delta Kappan*, 65(2), 102.

Nichols, R. (1987, January). *The negative side of technology in education*. Paper presented at the annual meeting of The Association for Educational Communication and Technology, Atlanta.

Piaget, J. (1970). *Structuralism*. New York: Harper & Row.

Piaget, J. (1973). *To understand is to invent: The future of education*. New York: Grossman.

Piaget, J. (1976). *The grasp of consciousness*. Cambridge, MA: Harvard University Press.

Piaget, J. (1977). *The development of thought: Equilibration of cognitive structures*. New York: Viking Press.

Piaget, J. (1978). *Success and understanding*. Cambridge, MA: Harvard University Press.

Piaget, J. (1980). *Experiments in contradiction*. Chicago: University of Chicago Press.

Rico, G. L. (1983). *Writing the natural way*. Los Angeles: J. P. Tarcher.

Risley, W. (1986, January). Keynote address at the annual meeting of The Association for Educational Communication and Technology, Las Vegas.

Romanish, B. (1987, May/June). A skeptical view of educational reform. *Journal of Teacher Education*, 38(3), 9–12.

Rorty, R. (1979). *Philosophy and the mirror of nature*. Princeton, NJ: Princeton University Press.

Rowe, M. B. (1986, January/February). Wait time: Slowing down may be a way of speeding up! *Journal of Teacher Education, 37*(1), 43–50.

Rowland, S. (1984). *The enquiring classroom.* London: Falmer Press.

Sexton, A. (1961). From the garden. *All my pretty ones.* Boston: Houghton-Mifflin.

Sigel, I. E. (1978). Constructivism and teacher education. *The Elementary School Journal, 78*(5), 333–338.

Simon, M. (1985). *A model for teacher education programs.* Unpublished manuscript, University of Massachusetts, Amherst.

Simon, M. A., & Schifter, D. (1988). *Teacher education from a constructivist perspective: The Educational Leaders in Mathematics project* (National Science Foundation Grant Report no. TEI-8552391). South Hadley, MA: Mt. Holyoke College.

Smith, B. O. (1980). Pedagogical education: How about reform? *Phi Delta Kappan, 62*(2), 87–93.

Steffe, L. P., & Cobb, P. (1988). *Construction of arithmetical meanings and strategies.* New York: Springer-Verlag.

Waddington, C. H. (1975). *The evolution of an evolutionist.* Ithaca, NY: Cornell University Press.

Wadsworth, B. (1978). *Piaget for the classroom teacher.* New York: Longman.

Walter, N. W. (1962). *Let them write poetry.* New York: Holt, Rinehart and Winston.

White, E. B. (1952). *Charlotte's Web.* New York: Harper & Row.

Wiggins, S. (1986). Revolution in the teaching profession: A comparative review of two reform reports. *Educational Leadership, 44*(2), 56–59.

Winkler, K. J. (1987, October 7). Interdisciplinary research: How big a challenge to traditional fields? *The Chronicle of Higher Education,* pp. A2–A15.

Index

About the Author

Catherine Twomey Fosnot is Assistant Professor of Education and coordinator of the sixth-year program, Classroom Teacher Specialist, at Southern Connecticut State University in New Haven. In 1986, while on leave from SCSU, she worked on the Summermath for Teachers project at Mount Holyoke College. She is past President of the Association for Constructivist Teaching, and in 1984 she received the ERIC/ECTJ Young Scholar Award for her writing on the topic of constructivism and educational technology.